Sophocles: Philoctetes

DUCKWORTH COMPANIONS
TO GREEK AND ROMAN TRAGEDY

Series editor: Thomas Harrison

Euripides: Hippolytus
Sophie Mills

Euripides: Medea
William Allan

Seneca: Phaedra
Roland Mayer

Seneca: Thyestes
P.J. Davis

Sophocles: Ajax
Jon Hesk

Sophocles: Electra
Michael Lloyd

Sophocles: Philoctetes
Hanna M. Roisman

Sophocles: Women of Trachis
Brad Levett

DUCKWORTH COMPANIONS
TO GREEK AND ROMAN TRAGEDY

Sophocles: Philoctetes

Hanna M. Roisman

Duckworth

First published in 2005 by
Gerald Duckworth & Co. Ltd.
90-93 Cowcross Street, London EC1M 6BF
Tel: 020 7490 7300
Fax: 020 7490 0080
inquiries@duckworth-publishers.co.uk
www.ducknet.co.uk

ISBN 0 7156 3384 8

Typeset by Ray Davies

Contents

For
Yossi Roisman, Elad Roisman,
and Shalev Roisman

Preface

Like other classical Greek tragedies, written over 2,400 years ago, Sophocles' *Philoctetes* is an extraordinary and timeless play. Dramatising the efforts of people who had wronged the play's hero, Philoctetes, to induce him to join the Greek forces in their war against Troy, the tragedy traces the moral and emotional development of the young Neoptolemus as he struggles between the values of honesty and subterfuge, honour and expedience.

This book, written mainly for students and non-professionals, aims to help readers with limited familiarity with the classical world and its literature to better appreciate and enjoy the play. It discusses Greek theatre and performance, the mythical background of the play, and the literary, intellectual and political context in which it was written and first performed. The book tries to illuminate Sophocles' means of shaping plot and character as well as the ways in which he grapples with the intellectual and political developments of his day. It provides analyses of the three main characters, and highlights the play's complexities and ambiguities. The aim is to combine depth of analysis with clarity and accessibility. Hopefully, some of the points will also be of interest to scholars.

I owe thanks first to the generations of students who have studied Greek drama with me, both at Tel Aviv University and at Colby College, whether in Greek or in translation. It is their scrutiny and questioning that led me to consider this play and tragedy as a whole from fresh points of view. I owe special gratitude to a group of people who have been a stout support to me in recent years. I wish to thank Dr Toby Mostysser both for making the manuscript more readable and for her probing questions, insights and comments. I thank Karen Gillum for her close reading of the manuscript. I also thank Tom Harrison and the anonymous referee for their helpful comments, and Deborah Blake for her encouragement and facilitation. I am grateful to the Classics Department at Cornell University, which extended to me the courtesy of office space and the use of its exhaustive Olin library. I thank the members of the department for the warm welcome they gave me. Special thanks are due to John Coleman and Jeff Rusten who have made their offices available to me during my sabbatical year and summers. I also thank Bea Rosenberg and Zeev and Nadia Rubinsohn for their steadfast encouragement. And last but not least, I am grateful to the dedicated team of librarians at the interlibrary loan department of Miller Library at Colby College who spared no efforts in getting me any article or book I requested. My deepest thanks are to my husband Yossi Roisman and my sons Elad and Shalev Roisman, on whom I can always rely and to whom this book is dedicated.

1

Theatre and Performance

It seems appropriate to begin this introduction to *Philoctetes* with a note of caution: we have relatively few certainties about fifth-century Greek drama. *Philoctetes* is one of only seven extant plays by Sophocles, out of an opus of over 120 works. Sophocles (496-406 BCE) himself is one of only three classical Greek dramatists, along with Aeschylus (525-456 BCE) and Euripides (480-406 BCE), whose plays have survived at all. The many others who wrote tragedies have left only their names.[1]

The fate of the theatre or theatres where the plays were performed is similar. We know from various records that *Philoctetes*, like the other extant tragedies, was performed at the City Dionysia (or Great Dionysia) of Athens. This was the largest and most magnificent of Athens' annual state-sponsored religious festivals. By the time the *Philoctetes* was performed, it had become a major Greek festival with an international audience, second only to the Olympics.[2] Held in late March, it celebrated the life and deeds of Dionysus, the god of wine and vegetation, along with the coming of spring. In the fifth century BCE, no play was mounted for more than a single performance at this festival. Although popular plays were reproduced in local *deme* (township) theatres in the fifth century, as well as in Athens throughout the following century, most plays probably saw only one performance in all, a fact that helps to explain why so few have come down to us.

The plays were put on several days into the festival, as part of formal competitions. Three days were allotted to the tragic competition, one to the comic. On each of the three days of the tragic competition, a different playwright mounted three tragedies (a trilogy), followed by a satyr play. The trilogies could follow a single story or tell different stories, as most probably did. We do not know with what other plays *Philoctetes* was produced or what position it occupied in its trilogy.

The dramatic performances were preceded by several days of ceremony and celebration in which the whole community participated, along with foreign visitors and dignitaries. On the day before the performances, the statue of Dionysus was escorted to the theatre, where it remained for the duration of the festival, in a procession accompanied by priests and young men of military age. Animal sacrifices were made at Dionysus' temple, behind the theatre, and offerings to the god were carried in a procession which included women and resident foreigners. Athenian men carried leather bottles filled with wine or long thin loaves of bread, foreign residents wore purple robes and carried trays of other offerings. The plays' producers, termed *chorêgoi*, paraded in magnificent robes of gold and purple. After the sacrifices there were choral competitions for men and boys. In the evening, men took to the streets, accompanied by torchbearers and musicians. These festivities, and the plays that followed, served to display Athens' wealth, power, and talent.

Like the rest of the festival, the tragedies were sponsored by the state. Playwrights who wished to show their plays had to submit them to the *archon eponymos*, a high-ranking official, who selected the three tragedians for the year from among the many applicants. For each playwright, the *archon eponymos* selected a *chorêgos*, literally chorus leader, but in effect a producer, who had to foot most of the bill for the productions,[3] and (later in the century) probably the lead actors as well. If a playwright were unlucky, he might be matched with a miserly *chorêgos* and less talented actors. From the mid-fifth century on, the state paid the lead actors and the tragedians. While the playwrights were not quite state employees, it is clear that they were not independent of the state either. It is unlikely that a tragedian would have been able to mount a play that displeased the *archon eponymos*.

From the plays that survive, we know that the state's involvement did not have the stultifying effect one might expect, either artistically or intellectually. Being state-sponsored, the plays had a strong didactic element. They familiarised the public with the myths that comprised their cultural heritage and engaged them in considering the myths' meanings and implications. They also clearly supported the democratic values of fifth-century Athens, among other ways through their repeated denunciations of tyranny and tyrants.[4] But they are subtle, nuanced, often ambiguous, and allow for a range of views on every issue they raise. The involvement of the state seems to have ensured that the issues that were treated were of public interest. It also probably defined the outer boundaries to the questioning and criticism that appear in many of the plays.[5]

Above all, the plays had to please the huge Athenian audiences, estimated at between 15,000 and 20,000 spectators, from all strata of society. The first few rows of the theatre were occupied by the elite: the priest of Dionysus, the Athenian magistrates, and visiting ambassadors from various states.[6] Most of the audience, however, were ordinary Athenian citizens. Since citizenship was restricted to adult males, it probably consisted mainly of men. Boys attended with their slave-tutors. Whether or not women were allowed to attend the performances is a matter of contention. The traditional view is that women were barred from attending the tragic and comic performances alike; recent scholarship argues that they were admitted to the tragic performances.[7] Although the evidence is inconclusive, the fact that so many of the tragedies feature women as key characters and deal sympathetically with their

11

concerns lends support to the latter view. At some point –
whether in the fifth century or the fourth – subsidies became
available for those who could not afford the price, making it
easier for the *dêmos*, or masses, to attend.[8] Dissatisfied spectators were known to express their opinions by clapping,
whistling, kicking the seats with their heels, shouting insults,
or throwing food at the actors. Though violence in the theatre
was severely penalised, this sort of behaviour was apparently
acceptable.[9]

Audience preferences may also have been considered in the
selection of the tragedians who would participate in the festivals and in the evaluation of their plays for the competitions.
The management of the festival was subject to review, and
complaints could be made.[10] Thus, while the *archon eponymos*
could select the participating playwrights as he saw fit, he also
had to be able to justify his selection in case of objection.

As for the competition, the plays were evaluated by a panel
of judges formed through a combination of selection and lot. The
judges were probably chosen on the basis of some criteria of
education and discernment. Yet the documentation that has
come down to us contains telltale grumbling that the judges
were often swayed or intimidated by the reactions of the audience.[11] Put differently, it tells us that the winning playwrights
were those who were likely to have been appreciated by the
ordinary folk as well. From the public records of the plays, we
can calculate that Sophocles (and his *chorêgoi*) won some
twenty first prizes in the 62-year course of his career, some of
them in competition with Aeschylus or Euripides, and many
seconds. To our knowledge, he never came third.

Thus, even though classical Greek drama was state-supported,
we can surmise that it was popular drama, in the best sense of
the term: that it was written for the entire polis and that it
moved and addressed the concerns of the ordinary Athenian.

Performances took place in the open air and in daylight at

1. Theatre and Performance

the Theatre of Dionysus, on the south-east slopes of the Acropolis. The performing area, a large space termed the *orchêstra* (dancing place), was located on a levelled space at the bottom of the hillside. The shape of the *orchêstra* is in dispute. Some scholars, basing their surmise on the remains of the stone theatre begun by Lycurgus in the late 330s BCE, maintain that it was circular.[12] Others suggest that it was a rectangle or trapezoid, as were some of the contemporary *deme* (township) theatres. The scarcity of remains and problems of dating and interpreting them make certainty impossible. What can be deduced is that the *orchêstra* had to be large enough to accommodate the fifty-member choruses that competed in the festival on the days before the dramatic competitions. Also in dispute is whether there was an elevated stage for the actors in the fifth century or whether they would have played their parts from the *orchêstra* itself. If there was a stage when *Philoctetes* was produced in 409 BCE, it was probably still no more than a raised narrow wooden platform about a metre high and connected to the *orchêstra* by several steps in the centre.

Behind the playing area stood a stage-building, about twelve metres long and four metres high. It was termed the *skênê*, after its origins as a tent or hut. When *Philoctetes* was produced, this too was probably still a temporary wooden structure that could be removed after the festival. The action of the Greek tragedies took place in the outdoor space in front of the stage-building, with off-stage actions occurring within the building. The structure represented whatever edifice the play referred to (e.g. palace, temple, cottage, cave, etc.). It had a doorway in the centre and possibly two smaller doors, one at each side, which served as entrance/exit between the outdoor and indoor spaces. The inside of the stage-building served as a changing room for the actors and a storage space. On either side of the *orchêstra* and running up to the stage-building were two broad aisles, usually referred to as *eisodoi* or *parodoi,* which served as en-

13

trances for the Chorus and characters arriving from the outside. The pathways could also be used by the spectators.

The seating area, or auditorium, was large enough to hold 15,000 to 20,000 spectators. Its shape, like that of the *orchêstra*, is a matter of debate. Some scholars envision a horseshoe-shape, with seating surrounding the playing area on three sides, others a rectangular shape, with rectilinear seating, possibly curving at the ends. In either case, the seating would have been arrayed in tiers, rising with the hillside, and giving most spectators a pretty full – if distant – view of the action.

Stage furniture for ancient productions was minimal. According to Aristotle (*Poetics* 1449a16), Sophocles introduced scene painting (*skênographia*).[13] Whether the painting was done on cloth draped over the stage-building or on wooden panels placed or hung in front of it is not known. In either case, most of the audience would not have been able to see details. The painting thus probably depicted little more than the type of location (e.g. urban, rural, seashore) and the type of edifice the stage-building represented.

The staging possibilities were expanded by mechanical devices, of which two, the *ekkyklêma* and the *mêchanê*, have a bearing on *Philoctetes*. The *ekkyklêma* was a wooden platform on wheels, some 2.5 x 1.5 metres. It was positioned in the central doorway of the stage building, but it could be moved about. The *mêchanê*, or crane, consisted of a wheel hanging on a hook fixed to the left side of the stage-building. By turning the wheel, the dramatist could lower a god or statue of a god to the stage or roof of the stage-building – which gave rise to the well-known Latin phrase *deus ex machina*: the god from the machine, to describe implausible endings to stories in which all the problems are resolved by divine appearance.

Greek tragedies can be described as verse musicals. Song and dance, accompanied mostly by pipe music, are essential components, along with spoken speech and recitative (declamatory song or chanting accompanied by the music of the pipes). The entire script is in verse. Every Greek tragedy featured a Chorus, of at first twelve, later fifteen members, who danced and sang. Scenes are generally separated by antiphonal choral odes termed *stasima*. The choral songs and monodies (lyric solos), both accompanied by a double reed flute, were written in a great variety of metres and rhythms. The characters spoke mostly in iambic trimeter, which, according to Aristotle, is the metre closest to the spoken cadence (*Poetics* 1449a19). Songs or recitative punctuate the spoken dialogue and monologues throughout a tragedy. In *Philoctetes*, songs make up around thirty per cent of the lines.

The structure of Greek tragedy is formal and fairly predictable. The play typically begins with a *prologos* (prologue), spoken by a god or one or two of the characters, which sets the scene and provides the background to the action. The *prologos* comes to an end with the first choral utterance, or *parodos* ('accompanying song'), and usually marks the Chorus' entrance. In addition to providing more background information, the *parodos* generally strikes the play's key emotional chord. In *Philoctetes*, this is pathos in the form of pity for the suffering hero. The *parodos* is followed by three to five *epeisodia* (episodes or scenes). They consist mainly of spoken dialogue between characters or recitatives between a character and the Chorus, but also may contain lyrical passages, lamentations, or incidental songs by the Chorus. The action is brought to a height and the tensions resolved in the *exodos*, which is in effect the last scene. The play generally ends with a choral song, sung as the Chorus exits the *orchêstra*.[14]

The tragedians also tended to observe conventions of plot and character. Almost all the plots were based on myth. The main characters were larger-than-life mythical figures, usually great warriors or members of ruling houses. Some had divine ancestry, some the special interest of a god. The Chorus could consist

15

of people from any walk of life, from the king's counsellors through ordinary folk. They provide information, comment on the action, and sometimes participate in the action as well. Their comments are to be taken as the normative view, that is the view held by most people or by most people in their position, which may or may not have been the view that the playwright wished to advance.[15] The action, as Aristotle would observe a century later, was generally compressed into the span of a day. It was also usually restricted to a single place. Though there were exceptions to both conventions, their implication was that the action of the play was generally the culmination of events before the play started, which the playwright had to relate to the audience without boring them.[16] Violence was generally not displayed on stage, but usually recounted by the Chorus or a messenger, who, in addition to telling what happened, would convey the horror, grief, or other emotion that the violence evoked.

Both the actors and the Chorus wore masks, which completely covered their heads front and back, with openings only for the eyes and mouth.[17] The masks were generally made of linen or some other simple material, covered in plaster and painted. The mouth was open wide to provide a clear outlet for the actor's voice and help his enunciation.[18] The whites of the eyes were painted on, but the place for the pupils hollowed out so the actor could see. Hair, skin colour and facial expression (usually gloomy, fierce, or sad) varied with the character. The convention was pale masks for women, darker masks for men. The colouring could be manipulated to suggest that a man was effeminate or a woman masculine, or a particularly pale mask could be used for a character who was ill or dead.[19] It is not known to what extent masks depicted general character types or roles, or were distinctly individual, portraying particular personalities. Nor is it known how naturalistic the masks were, though it seems likely that the features would have been enlarged, and possibly exaggerated, so that they could be seen from a distance.

From vase paintings we know that tragic costume consisted of a tunic and two mantles, one long and one short, and was worn by nearly all the characters.[20] The tunic was a long flowing robe, fastened by a broad girdle under the breast, with folds usually draping down to the feet and long sleeves reaching to the waist. The long mantle, the *himation*, passed around the right shoulder and covered most of the body. The shorter one, the *chlamys*, was worn over the left shoulder.

In its components, the tragic costume resembled the clothing worn off-stage. It was raised above the everyday, however, by its richness and sumptuousness. The tunics worn by most of the key characters had ample draping and elaborate designs, and their mantles were brightly coloured – which, it may be noted, also contributed to the actors' visibility. Although no attempt was made at historical realism, which was irrelevant to the plays, efforts seem to have been made to dress the characters in accordance with their roles. Attendants and minor characters wore shorter tunics and less colourful mantles. Some character categories had special identifying marks. Kings were outfitted with a crown and sceptre. Individual characters also came on stage with identifying markers. Apollo carried his bow, and Hermes his magic wand, for example. Philoctetes was dressed in rags.[21] Heracles, being a god, would probably have been dressed more sumptuously than Odysseus and Neoptolemus.

Early Greek tragedies were performed with two speaking actors and one or two non-speaking mutes. Aristotle credits Sophocles with adding a third speaking actor (*Poetics* 1449a16).[22] The lead actor was termed the *protagonist*, the second the *deuteragonist*, the third, the *tritagonist*. Since the tragedies routinely had more characters than actors, actors would play more than one role. The use of masks was obviously an advantage here.

Of all the qualities required of an actor, the most important was a strong and versatile voice.[23] The huge size and open-air venue of the Theatre of Dionysus meant that the actors would have had to project very well in order to be heard. To play multiple roles, they needed to have voices versatile enough to endow each character – of whatever age or gender – with his or her distinct vocal signature. The doubling-up of roles would have required a versatile voice even if there was some degree of specialisation (e.g. with certain actors playing for certain trage-dians and certain actors possibly being tagged for certain parts, such as the king or women). Moreover, versatility of voice would also have been required to compensate for the limitations cre-ated by the use of masks and the nature of the costumes. The actors wore the same mask with the same fixed expression throughout either the whole or most of the play. As a result, facial expression could not be used to convey emotion at all, and gesture only to a limited extent.

The key actor, the protagonist, was not necessarily the one with the greatest number of lines, but the one whose part required the greatest flexibility of voice. He was expected to manage all the metres: the sung lyrics, the recitative and the spoken metres. The second and third actors were given only recitatives and spoken lines. Tradition has it that Sophocles had to give up acting in his plays early in his career for lack of a sufficiently strong voice. It is also said that he often wrote for the actor Tlepolemos so as to draw on his performing strength and singing ability.[24]

So how was *Philoctetes* staged? The Greek tragedies have come down to us without stage directions.[25] The first written texts were probably scripts for the actors, and only later were popular plays transcribed for reproduction. Since the poets directed – and often acted in – their own plays, and were on the spot to give instructions, written stage directions would have served no purpose. So the plays' staging is a matter of surmise,

18

based on the verbal scene-painting that the poets provided for their audiences. In the following account, I try to point out both what the audience may have seen (i.e. the staging) and what they were asked to imagine from Sophocles' verbal clues.

In the *Philoctetes*, Odysseus begins to paint the scene in the first two lines, as he tells Neoptolemus that Lemnos is 'surrounded by water' and 'untrod by humankind and uninhabited'. Since the playing area was pretty bare in all Greek plays, the description tells the spectators that the empty stage in this case really did represent a bare and deserted place.

Further scene-painting is provided in lines 16 to 21, as Odysseus instructs Neoptolemus to look for a cave with two mouths, one in the sun, the other a shady tunnelled passage, not far from a spring, and in lines 26-7, where Neoptolemus identifies the cave as Philoctetes' habitation. Since the cave serves as the indoor space in this play, we may surmise that the painted backdrop mounted on or in front of the stage-building depicted a cave and the mountain or rocks in which it was situated. The door at the centre of the stage-building would probably have been taken as the cave's seaward entrance. The other entrance would probably have been out of sight, perhaps connected to the seaward entrance by the tunnel.[26] Further information is provided a few lines later, when Neoptolemus, having found the cave, informs Odysseus that it is up 'above' (29) and goes on to describe its contents.

Thus far, we can deduce that Odysseus and Neoptolemus, coming from their ship or ships, probably entered the *orchêstra* from one of the side aisles. The audience would have imagined their ship(s) anchored out of sight at the end of the aisle. We can further deduce that when Neoptolemus went looking for the cave, he probably mounted the steps at the centre of the actors' platform (assuming there was one) and that Odysseus either climbed up with him or soon followed.

From the *parodos*, we learn that Philoctetes' cave is at 'the edge' of the island (144). This detail is elaborated in lines 1000 and 1002, when Philoctetes, standing, we may presume, in front of his cave, refers to 'the rock above' and threatens to jump off it. This suggests that Philoctetes' cave is located near an elevated precipice which the spectators are asked to imagine. They may or may not have been helped to do so by positioning the *ekkyklêma*, possibly decked out with some large rocks, in front of the cave.

There is some uncertainty about the timing of the Chorus' entrance into the *orchêstra*. Traditionally the Chorus entered as they recited the *parodos* at the end of the *prologos*. In the *Philoctetes*, the Chorus' description of Philoctetes as a 'suspicious man' (137), their concern that he might attack them (156), and their description of his loneliness, unhappiness and pain (169-90) are not based on anything Neoptolemus tells them. Rather, they seem to be extrapolations from information that Odysseus had given to Neoptolemus in the *prologos*. It is hard to see how the Chorus could say what they do without having been present then. On the other hand, to our knowledge, neither the tragedians nor their audiences were overly concerned with this level of realism.[27] In any case, once the Chorus entered the *orchêstra*, they invariably remained until the end of the play.[28]

The direction from which Philoctetes enters the playing area (220) is also uncertain. The Chorus' preceding remark about hearing a man treading 'on the path' (206) and their conjecture that he may have stopped 'to look at the inhospitable harbour' (218) would seem to indicate that Philoctetes came along one of the side aisles, much as Odysseus and Neoptolemus had done.[29] Several scholars, however, propose that he came on through the stage-building, having entered the cave from its landward entrance, not seen from the auditorium.[30] This claim would make sense in light of the emphasis placed on his cave having two mouths.

1. Theatre and Performance

There is less uncertainty about Heracles' entrance at the end of the *Philoctetes*. As a god who suddenly appears before the human protagonists with no prior notice, the only way he could have come is by the *mêchanê*. Where he stands, however, is open to question. In principle, his position could be on the roof of the *skênê*, on the *ekkyklêma-cum*-cliff, or on the stage platform itself, level with Neoptolemus and Philoctetes.

About the assignment of the actors in *Philoctetes*, the scholarly assumption is that Philoctetes was played by the protagonist, Neoptolemus by the deuteragonist, and Odysseus, the Trader, and Heracles by the third actor. Philoctetes' antiphonal singing with the Chorus would have required a good solo voice and one strong enough to stand out clearly from the choral group. Whether the second or third actor played Neoptolemus, however, is open to debate. It is difficult to know whether playing Odysseus, the Trader, and Heracles – largely spoken parts with little emotional variation – or Neoptolemus, whose position and moods change in the course of the play, would have required the greater skill and flexibility of voice.[31]

Classical Greek tragedy was formal, stylised and consciously removed from the everyday. The masks and costumes identified the plays as tragedies, as opposed to comedies, and as dramas, as opposed to depictions of 'real life'. Along with the minimalist scenery and props, the formal structure, and the mythological background, they announced that the events portrayed took place in another realm, beyond the mundane.

As such, the kinds of naturalistic details that may be of concern to modern audiences, and for that matter to some scholars, seem not to have mattered to the ancient playwrights and their audiences. To take just one example, some modern critics are baffled by the question whether Odysseus and Neoptolemus reached Lemnos in the same ship or separate ones.[32] A clear answer to this question would shed light on whether or not Neoptolemus is telling the truth on the two occasions when he promises to take Philoctetes home instead of to Troy. If there is only one ship, Odysseus', then Neoptolemus is clearly lying. Yet the play is quite vague on this detail, which is unlikely to have been the case had it really mattered. Much the same can be said with regard to such questions as how the Chorus knew that Philoctetes was a 'suspicious' man before Neoptolemus told them, or what Neoptolemus knew about Helenus' prophecy at various points in the play.

In contrast to modern audiences, who, accustomed to television, passively absorb what is put before them, the ancient Greek audiences who filled the Theatre of Dionysus would have had to be active viewers. They would have needed to make an imaginative leap from the painted backdrop to Philoctetes' cave in the mountains; from the *ekkyklêma* to the pinnacle from which Philoctetes threatened to throw himself. They would have had to visualise the bareness of the island and the details of Philoctetes' cave from Odysseus' and Neoptolemus' minimalist descriptions. The spectators would have had to participate in 'making' the scene for themselves.

The ancient Greek audience may also have focused on the words and ideas of the drama more than their modern counterparts generally do. The verbal scene-painting and the extensive background information would have required the audience's attention to relevant verbal detail. Relegating violence to behind the scenes and the constraints on the actors' movements would have reduced the distractions that turn modern audiences away from words and ideas. The sparseness of the scenery may have had a similar effect. At the same time, the dance and the music of the tragedies, no longer extant, would have augmented the emotional power of the words.

The conventions of classical Greek tragedy seem to have enabled an optimal wedding of thought and emotion, both brought to a pitch of intensity. Judging from the large attendance at the tragic performances year after year, from the reproduction of plays in the *deme* theatres and their revival in the fourth century, and from written evidence, the Athenian audiences appreciated the tragedies and were greatly moved by them. We know that *Philoctetes* was a popular play, well thought of and meaningful to the ancient Greek audience, not only because the trilogy it was in won first prize in the tragic competition, but also simply because it has come down to us. Its survival means that the text was copied and the play reproduced.[33]

2

The Myth

There is something a bit anomalous in writing about the mythical background of Greek tragedy. True, almost all the Greek tragedies drew on well-known myths for their plots and characters. Their characters are heroes or heroines from the mythical past, their plots are based on mythical exploits, and both characters and action are invested with the primal quality that is inherent in myth. Audiences were familiar with the myths, much as some people today are familiar with the key biblical stories. The better educated probably knew more variants of the myths, and possibly the more obscure ones, but even the less educated would have been familiar with the key myths. Yet much of what we know of Greek mythology today comes, in addition to Roman sources, from the tragedies themselves, and not from the tragedians' sources. With the notable exception of Homer's *Iliad* and *Odyssey*, which in any case do not treat many of the myths used by the fifth-century tragedians, most of the possible sources have been lost. Whether this is because texts have not survived or because the bulk of the mythic lore was oral, we do not know. The better part of what has come down to us is from texts written centuries later. Thus, when scholars write of the mythical background of *Philoctetes*, or of any other Greek tragedy, what they really mean is the myth, in its multiple versions, that *may* have been available to the playwright. What scholars present is actually a reconstruction based not on direct evidence but on a diversity of clues.

Complicating matters is the fact that, in contrast to the

Bible, Greek myth was not sacred. It was not conceived of as divine truth or even as holy. While fifth-century Athenian law punished disrespect for the gods, there were no doctrinal requirements, certainly not with regard to the human and part-mortal, part-divine personae of the myths and their exploits. This freedom from doctrine resulted in the mythology being rather loose. There was no such thing as 'the myth' in the sense of a fixed canonical story. Most myths seem to have had a fixed core, and around that multiple variants. Freedom from doctrine also permitted considerable leeway in the depiction of mythical personae and their stories at different times and by different authors.

For the ancient playwrights, myth posed challenges and provided opportunities. The main challenge was to flesh out the basic story in a way that was interesting and convincing. These challenges can be readily illustrated with the Philoctetes myth. The kernel of this myth is that Odysseus and the other Greeks abandoned Philoctetes on the island of Lemnos after he was bitten by a snake and left him there suffering from his unhealed wound, while they fought the Trojans. Then, some ten years later, it was prophesied that they would not be able to defeat Troy without Philoctetes and the unerring arrows of Heracles that he possessed. Odysseus returned to the island to fetch him. Philoctetes went to Troy and helped vanquish the city. These elements of the myth are givens.

The playwrights who used the Philoctetes myth, however, had to conceive of a convincing dynamic by which Odysseus got Philoctetes to go Troy to fight beside the men who had so mistreated him. They would have had to ask themselves questions such as: How would Philoctetes have felt after having been abandoned to his suffering by his comrades? How would he have received Odysseus? What stratagems or arguments would Odysseus have used? What could have brought Philoctetes to leave Lemnos for Troy? Each playwright would have to find answers with sufficient psychological realism to make his rendition of the myth convincing.

Moreover, if there were any previous plays on the myth he chose, the playwright would have had to take these into consideration. He would have had to distinguish his rendition, both to avoid boring the audience with repetition and to put his own imprint on the material. Plays on the Philoctetes myth had been produced by Aeschylus and Euripides before Sophocles produced his. Though this does not necessarily mean that Sophocles actually created his version after they did theirs – his career overlapped with both of theirs, and there is nothing to say that he did not conceive his play many years before it was actually produced – the likelihood is that he did. He would then have had to draw his characters differently from theirs and present different interactions.

The opportunities provided by the myth were the inverse of the challenges. The opportunities stemmed from the need to build on the ready plots and repertoire of familiar personages provided by the myths. Each playwright had to transform the mythical personages into stage characters, with their own motives, personalities and ways of speaking. Each had to conceive of the interactions that would bring the mythic events to life, invest the interactions with dramatic tension, and make the unfolding of the events emotionally plausible. These inherent requirements of drama were precisely what allowed each dramatist to express his own vision and purposes, while the expectation that every playwright would offer his own variation on the myths must have encouraged each to wrestle with the material anew and to come up with a fresh interpretation of the characters, their deeds and the meaning of the events.

At the same time, earlier dramatic renditions of a myth may have enabled the dramatist to engage in a dialogue with his predecessors and also to build on and play with audience expectations. Whether Sophocles actually did these things in his

2. The Myth

Philoctetes is debated by scholars.[1] The fact that Sophocles' play was produced twenty-two years after Euripides' *Philoctetes* and even more years after Aeschylus' would make such a dialogue seem unlikely. Much of the audience would have changed, and how many of those who had seen the earlier productions would have remembered the details is open to question. On the other hand, in the absence of evidence to the contrary, we cannot rule out the possibility that Euripides' and Aeschylus' plays were performed in other venues in the interim, which means that the audience may have known and been able to consider Sophocles' play in relation to theirs.

Sophocles' *Philoctetes*, like every other classical Greek tragedy, can be enjoyed and understood without knowledge of the mythic background. In the prologue to the play, Odysseus tells Neoptolemus everything that the audience needs to know of the story: that Philoctetes is the son of Poeas, that Odysseus had marooned him on the deserted isle of Lemnos with a suppurating wound in his foot (5-7); and that Odysseus has come to take Philoctetes back to Troy because the city cannot be conquered without Philoctetes' bow (54-69). These key details are repeated and elaborated in the *parodos* and in Philoctetes' account to Neoptolemus (197-8, 254-84). The dialogue in the prologue also informs the audience of what they must know about Neoptolemus: that he is Achilles' son and that Odysseus needs his help to bring Philoctetes to Troy; similarly, too, Neoptolemus' noble lineage is repeated and elaborated on in the young man's first conversation with Philoctetes (239-41). These are the basic details of the myth, or myths, that the audience needs to know to follow the action and to understand the dynamic between the characters. Because they are important to the play, Sophocles makes sure to provide them, not once but twice.

So why would we want to trouble with the mythic background if Sophocles provides it? The answer is that in all likelihood the better educated spectators in ancient Athens knew other variants of the myth.[2] They might have known of Aeschylus' or Euripides' productions, read poems in which the incident features, or heard other versions. They would also have been familiar with the characters. Their knowledge would have enabled them to better appreciate the possibilities that were available to Sophocles and the choices he made. It may do the same for us.

Much of our knowledge of the myths comes from sources that postdate the playwright. We cannot rule out the possibility that elements found in later writings were available earlier, and there is reason to believe that some of them probably were. But we cannot be certain that they were available to the playwright either. It is important to keep in mind how incomplete our knowledge is.

This chapter will look at several different types of references to the myth of Philoctetes and try to determine what these tell us about the mythical information that may have been available to Sophocles and about the choices he made. There is no attempt at a comprehensive analysis. The iconographic treatments are not discussed.[3] My hope is to convey the difficulties and uncertainties of exhuming the play's mythic background.[4]

The consideration of the key allusions will be followed by a more general discussion of the ways in which the major figures in the play may have been viewed in the fifth century. Most of the specific allusions to the myth focus on the action and tell very little about the personalities of the figures involved. Yet the personalities with which the playwrights endowed the mythic figures are what enabled the audience to identify with and be moved by them, and the playwrights to convey the themes and ideas they wished to relate. Just as they could draw on a mythic tradition for the action of their plays, the playwrights had at their disposal a rich storehouse of mythic material from which to flesh out their characters. The chapter will end with a brief look at elements of their lore that pertain to the personalities of Philoctetes, Neoptolemus, and Odysseus.

There are only three extant references to the Philoctetes myth that we know for certain predated Sophocles. Aeschylus' and Euripides' plays on the Philoctetes myth preceded Sophocles', but they have been lost and all we know of them is from later accounts, whose accuracy we cannot vouch for. The first extant pre-Sophoclean source is Homer's *Iliad*, a reference in the catalogue of the ships (*Iliad* 2.718-24). Noting Philoctetes' absence from the war, Homer highlights the wounded hero's special relation to the bow, his isolation and pain on the island of Lemnos following his snakebite, his abandonment there by the Greeks, and their subsequent need of him. All these elements feature in Sophocles' play. But Homer's brief account tells us nothing about why the Achaeans abandoned Philoctetes and only hints at the prophecy that would cause the Greeks to remember him.

The second set of references, even briefer, is found in the *Odyssey*. In Book 3, Nestor relates that Philoctetes has returned home safely (190). In Book 8 Odysseus admits that Philoctetes surpassed him in archery (219). Neither detail figures in the *Philoctetes*.

The third pre-Sophoclean reference we have is from Pindar's first Pythian, an ode to Hieron, written in 470 BCE. Praising this tyrant of Syracuse for going to war even though he was ill, Pindar compares Hieron's act to Philoctetes' fighting in Troy despite the pain of his wound (51-5). From this we learn that Philoctetes was instrumental in vanquishing Troy – a key 'fact' that Sophocles could rely on his audience to know.

Of the many post-Sophoclean references, we will consider three types. The first consists of two summaries written several centuries after Sophocles' time or at an unknown date. The second comprises two discourses in Greek by the philosopher and orator Dio Chrysostom (first century CE), from whom we learn something about Aeschylus' and Euripides' plays on the Philoctetes myth. The third comprises two Roman versions, one by Hyginus (64 BCE – 17 CE) and the other by Servius (second half of fourth century CE and early fifth century).[5]

The summaries are found in *Bibliotheca,* a compilation of myths wrongly attributed to Apollodorus (*fl.* 140 BCE) with the *Epitome,* an addendum to the *Bibliotheca,* consisting of surviving fragments from lost sections of the work, and in *The Epic Cycle,* ascribed to Lesches (?seventh century BCE). These provide information mainly about the elements of the myth that could have served as plot material, but leave no real clues as to how the important characters were viewed.

The fullest summary of the myth and the closest to Sophocles is from the *Epitome.* This tells that Philoctetes was bitten by a snake while performing a sacrifice to Apollo. It explains that Odysseus marooned Philoctetes on Lemnos at Agamemnon's orders, after his wound would not heal and the Argive soldiers could not endure the stench. It adds that, isolated on the island with the bow that he had inherited from Heracles, Philoctetes survived by shooting birds (*Epitome* 3.27). It then relates two prophecies and the actions that followed from them. The first prophecy, made by Calchas, was that the Greeks would not be able to capture Troy without Heracles' bow. The second, by Helenus, was that Troy would not be captured unless Pelops' bones were brought to the Greeks and Neoptolemus fought with them. In response to the first prophecy, it says, Odysseus went to Lemnos with Diomedes and induced Philoctetes to sail to Troy after having tricked him out of his bow. In response to the second, Odysseus and Phoenix were dispatched to Neoptolemus' grandfather Lycomedes on Scyros to persuade him to allow Neoptolemus to go, which he apparently did.

The Epic Cycle was summarised by Proclus (*c.* fifth century CE) and preserved in the ninth-century *Bibliotheca* of Photius, patriarch of Constantinople. It summarises four epics dealing with events before and after the plot of Homer's *Iliad*. The two summaries that refer to the Philoctetes story are of the *Cypria* and the *Little Iliad*, neither of which has survived. While the summaries postdate Sophocles, the epics themselves probably pre-date him. References to the Philoctetes myth are very brief. The summary of the *Cypria* mentions only the snakebite, stench and abandonment. The *Little Iliad*'s summary names Helenus as the seer who prophesied the taking of Troy, but gives no details. It also tells us that it is Diomedes who brings Philoctetes from Lemnos, and that, after Philoctetes' wound is healed and he kills Paris, Odysseus brings Neoptolemus from Scyros and gives him his father's arms.

So what do these brief accounts teach us about Sophocles' adaptation of the myth? For one thing, they suggest that Sophocles chose and adapted elements of the myth as he saw fit. He chose to connect the snakebite with the goddess Chryse and the sacrifice to Apollo rather than with a feast. While he has Philoctetes mention the foul odour of his wound, he has Odysseus skip over this detail and attribute the abandonment instead to orders from 'those in command' and justify those orders with the claim that Philoctetes' cries and groans brought bad luck at their religious rituals. He compacts the two voyages of Odysseus and Diomedes into one, chooses (like Aeschylus and Euripides before him) to dispatch Odysseus rather than Diomedes to Lemnos to fetch Philoctetes, and replaces Diomedes with Neoptolemus as Odysseus' lieutenant.

Why did Sophocles make these choices? Did he connect the snakebite to Chryse to make Philoctetes' suffering part of the divine scheme? Or, since we hear of the gods' involvement from the Chorus and Neoptolemus, did he want to suggest that these characters invoke the gods to excuse their own immoral actions? Did he have Odysseus speak of Philoctetes' disturbing the liturgies because he wanted to provide him with a somewhat more moral justification for abandoning Philoctetes than an unpleasant odour? Or did he want to suggest that Odysseus' rationalisation was distorted and self-serving? In dispatching Odysseus (rather than Diomedes) to Lemnos, Sophocles, like Aeschylus and Euripides, chose to dramatise the better known and also more controversial hero. But why did he involve Neoptolemus? Some answers are suggested in Chapter 4.

Another thing we may surmise from the summaries is that in the prevailing tradition Heracles was probably not involved in getting Philoctetes to leave Lemnos. While there is a certain risk in drawing conclusions from omission, the fact that Heracles is not mentioned in any of the summaries suggests that Sophocles invented this element of his play. This likelihood makes it incumbent on us to give Heracles' sudden appearance special thought.

Another omission of note is that none of the summaries relates in any detail how Odysseus averted Philoctetes' hostility or prevailed on him to leave Lemnos. Although Apollodorus' *Epitome* indicates that he used trickery, it says nothing about what his tricks were. Here it is of interest that Sophocles draws on elements both of this myth and of the related myth of Ajax to fill out the picture. He turns the tradition that Philoctetes' wound was healed in Troy into an inducement that Odysseus offers to get him to agree to go. He takes the Ajax myth, on which he had earlier written a play, and has Odysseus use it in his instructions to Neoptolemus about how to win Philoctetes' trust. In this myth, Ajax and Odysseus were rivals for the prize of Achilles' arms; Odysseus won them, according to Pindar undeservedly and dishonestly (*Nemean* 7.24-7; 8.23-7). Sophocles excises all reference to Ajax but has Odysseus direct Neoptolemus to tell Philoctetes that the Achaeans 'did not think you worthy of Achilles' arms' (62). We can see from these applications of mythic details (which are only two examples among many) something of the way in which Sophocles draws

from all parts of the mythic tradition to envision and dramatise
how his characters would act.

Finally, we may note that Sophocles does not refer to any of
the subsequent events in Troy, including Philoctetes' killing of
Paris or Neoptolemus' martial conduct there, which the summary of the *Little Iliad* treats in some detail. These omissions
enhance the play's coherence, help keep to a minimum the
'history' that has to be narrated in the prologue, and keep the
focus on Neoptolemus' conduct as a young man, before his acts
of brutality in the Trojan War.[6]

Two of Dio Chrysostom's discourses relate to the Philoctetes
plays. The fifty-second tells us something about the similarities
and differences between Sophocles' treatment of the myth and
the treatments of Aeschylus and Euripides.[7] The discourse is a
piece of literary criticism written for readers familiar with the
plays. The information it contains is thus both limited and
infused with Dio's subjectivity. It is nonetheless informative.
The key similarity seems to be in what Dio identifies as the
common theme in all three plays: 'the theft – or perhaps I
should say seizure – of Philoctetes' bow', and that Philoctetes
goes to Troy of his own free will but is also forced to go by
circumstances (52.2). The main difference that concerns him is
in the playwrights' styles (52.15).

Four other differences to which Dio points involve the playwrights' treatment of character, place, chorus and plot. He
describes Aeschylus' Odysseus as being the most earthy and
simple of the three, Euripides' as the most sophisticated, and
Sophocles' as kinder and gentler than Euripides'. Modern readers of the play do not see Sophocles' Odysseus as particularly
kind or gentle (see Chapter 5). Dio's evaluation suggests that
our judgment of Odysseus should perhaps be more tempered.

Dio indicates that Sophocles is the only one of the three
tragedians who made Lemnos a deserted island. In both
Aeschylus' and Euripides' versions it is populated. Expounding

on the implausibility of Philoctetes surviving for ten years without interacting with the island's residents, Dio implies that Sophocles' version was more plausible. Whether it is and whether such technical plausibility concerned fifth-century audiences are both debatable questions. Other explanations have been offered by modern scholars. Perhaps the most common is that in having the Greeks abandon Philoctetes on a deserted island, Sophocles was trying to accentuate Philoctetes' suffering and the Greeks' culpability.[8] Another is that the deserted island allowed Sophocles to portray Philoctetes as living in the most primitive state, before the development of society, and to show man's need for society, however flawed it is.[9]

Whatever the reason, the decision meant that the Chorus could not be the local inhabitants, as in Aeschylus' and Euripides' plays, but had to come to the island with Odysseus and Neoptolemus. As Dio points out, Sophocles' Chorus is made of those who sailed with them. This change had the advantage of avoiding the incongruity that Dio noted in the other two plays of the Choruses suddenly appearing after not having spoken to Philoctetes for the ten years that he lived in their midst.

Finally, Dio Chrysostom emphasises that Sophocles was the only one of the three playwrights to make Neoptolemus Odysseus' lieutenant. He implies that Aeschylus had Odysseus come alone and tells us that Euripides had him bring along Diomedes. He presents Sophocles' choice as a clever innovation and economical adaptation of the myth, in which, he explains, it was ordained that Neoptolemus and Philoctetes capture Troy together. There may be also other reasons for Sophocles' choice, however (see Chapter 4).

Dio Chrysostom's fifty-ninth discourse is a paraphrase of the prologue of Euripides' *Philoctetes*, originally produced in 431 BCE. How close to the original it is cannot be known, though its unflattering depiction of Odysseus as self-satisfied and callous is consistent with that in other Euripidean plays. The prologue consists of an opening monologue, in which Odysseus describes himself as motivated by the thirst for glory and willing to suffer hardship for it, followed by a dialogue with Philoctetes in which he pretends that he too is marooned and helpless on the island and asks for Philoctetes' help. His self-description is too self-laudatory to be genuinely flattering and makes him seem self-serving, and the tale he tells Philoctetes comes across as ugly against the truth of Philoctetes' genuine misery. Without the rest of the play, it would be precarious for us to compare Sophocles' Odysseus to Euripides'. We may, however, note that while Euripides' opening highlights the struggle between Odysseus and Philoctetes, Sophocles' opening highlights the struggle between Odysseus and Neoptolemos.

Hyginus' and Servius' accounts shift the moral balance from that implied in the accounts discussed above. Like the other renditions, Hyginus (*Fabulae* 102) tells of the awful smell of Philoctetes' wound, of Agamemnon's order to abandon Philoctetes on Lemnos, and of Odysseus (now termed Ulysses) going to fetch him when it was learned that Troy could not be captured without Heracles' arrows. However, it situates Philoctetes already in Lemnos when he was bitten, making the abandonment a less premeditated and possibly less reprehensible act than the other versions. It places the responsibility for the snakebite on Philoctetes himself by making it Juno's (Hera's) punishment for his having dared to light Heracles' funeral pyre. It presents Odysseus as inducing Philoctetes to leave Lemnos not by trickery but by promising to make him a king if he helps them to capture Troy. Philoctetes appears less innocent and Odysseus and the Greeks less blameworthy than in the versions discussed above.

The view of Philoctetes as culpable and the snakebite as a punishment also emerges in Servius' much later account. In his fourth- or fifth-century CE commentary on Virgil's *Aeneid* (3.420), Servius writes that Philoctetes had promised Heracles never to tell where his human remains were buried. But then, when it was learned that Heracles' arrows would be needed to take Troy, the Greeks pressured him to go back on his word. Though he refused to 'say' where Heracles was buried, he thumped on the gravesite with his foot. After that, Philoctetes went to the Trojan War and was injured by his own arrow in the same foot with which he had thumped. This account depicts Philoctetes as dishonourable, weak, a bit sneaky and decidedly unheroic.

Sophocles' play does not incorporate any of the details that are unique to Hyginus' and Servius' accounts. Whether this is because they were later additions and unavailable to him or because he chose to ignore them, we cannot know. What is relevant is the moral perspective these accounts bring to the story. Although Sophocles' play does not go so far as to blame Philoctetes for his plight or to exonerate Odysseus and the Greeks, it raises moral questions that do not arise from the simplest interpretation of the myth, blaming the Greeks for their offence against Philoctetes. Hyginus' and Servius' accounts highlight the wide range of possible interpretations of the myth.

Now we turn to indications of how the key characters in Sophocles' play may have been viewed in the fifth century. Philoctetes is the character to whose personality we have the fewest references. Those we have suggest that he may have been conceived either as a victim of his comrades' disloyalty and exploitation or as culpable for or contributing to his own suffering. The view of him as noble victim is sounded in Homer's description, as well as in Pindar's ode to Hieron (*Pythian* 1.51-5), though with greater emphasis on Philoctetes' heroism than his victimisation. Hyginus' *Fabulae* and Servius' comment, on the other hand, alert us to the potential for seeing Philoctetes as somewhat other than an entirely innocent victim.

Although we have no way of knowing how Philoctetes was

envisioned by Sophocles' contemporaries, the different accounts intimate that he was probably not seen as a one-dimensional figure. They suggest that in reading the play, we should be alert to nuances and ambiguity and to the possibility of some mix of nobility and culpability in his character.

Neoptolemus, it seems, may have been perceived either as a heroic warrior or as a brutal murderer. Both perceptions could readily have been deduced from his role in the last days of the Trojan War. As part of the Greek force, Neoptolemus was one of the heroes who helped to vanquish the city; and his killings, like those by the other Greeks, were the work of a warrior and a source of honour. However, several of the killings attributed to him were particularly terrible in that the victims were not soldiers, but persons who were defenceless and vulnerable and whom he killed in particularly horrible ways. These included Troy's aged king Priam, whom Neoptolemus killed at the altar of Zeus in the courtyard where he had sought protection, and the infant Astyanax, whom he hurled from the walls of Troy.[10]

The view of Neoptolemus as a noble and heroic warrior is salient in Book 11 of the *Odyssey*, where Odysseus, in his visit to the Otherworld, tells Achilles about his son's valour in the last days of Troy (*Odyssey* 11.505-37). In this account, Odysseus describes Neoptolemus both as a skilled speaker at the warriors' councils and an intrepid fighter, who killed innumerable fine warriors (*Odyssey* 11.516-22). Neoptolemus' eagerness to fight, his fearlessness and the slaughter he wrought are all to his credit.

The view of Neoptolemus as a brutal murderer appears in Virgil's *Aeneid*, written in the first century BCE, which expounds at length on his savagery (2.627-750). Comparing him to a snake fed on poisonous plants, Virgil describes how the brutal and degenerate warrior broke into the intimacy of the royal home and, 'insane with blood', slaughtered all who got in his way. Virgil describes his bloody murder of Priam's son

Polites in front of his parents, and his ruthless murder of Priam.

A more nuanced and ambivalent view than either of these is found in two of Pindar's odes, which recount Neoptolemus' death. In *Paean* 6, Pindar explains Neoptolemus' early death by Apollo's determination to avenge his killing of Priam as the latter sought sanctuary at Zeus' altar. While the ode notes Neoptolemus' aggression and violation of basic interdictions, it presents him mainly as a victim. *Nemean* 7, which does not mention Apollo's anger and says that Neoptolemos was killed in a quarrel over sacrificial meat, seems to have been aimed at correcting any negative impression left by the previous ode.

A nuanced view is also evident in Euripides' *Hecuba*, performed about 425. In this play, Neoptolemus is described as slashing the throat of Polyxena, the daughter of Priam and Hecuba, in a public execution after the sack of Troy. By nature, this is a brutal act and the entire play presents it as unjust. But the messenger, who may be considered a normative voice, does not present Neoptolemus as a brute, but tells that he was torn, 'both not wishing and wishing in pity of the maiden' (*Hecuba* 565). Overall, the play presents Neoptolemus as torn between his duty to his father (who demanded the sacrifice) and the state on the one hand, and his compassion on the other.

Sophocles too depicts Neoptolemus as torn between conflicting obligations and values, but also seems to manipulate the different perspectives of him. He depicts him as a young man before his brutal exploits at Troy, and makes only passing reference to them. Yet, there is an inherent tension in his choice of a mythic figure with a reputation for brutality to serve as his representative of youthful idealism and as a spokesman for pure heroic values. We may well wonder how Neoptolemus' objections to deceiving Philoctetes and his moments of compassion for him struck those in the audience who recalled him as the man who killed the aged Priam and his infant grandson, or how his reputation for brutality coloured the audience's assessment of his stated preference for using force, rather than deceit, to wrest Philoctetes' bow from him.

Odysseus was the most familiar of the three dramatis personae. There seems to have been an essential agreement in all the depictions that he was a consummate speaker and skilled trickster. The differences concern the moral appraisal of his penchant for deception. In Homer, Odysseus' ability to persuade and deceive was closely associated with his tremendous resourcefulness and consistently placed at the service of survival: his own, in the *Odyssey*, that of the Greek warriors in the *Iliad*. Its positive evaluation is evident throughout. It is distinctly expressed in Book 13 of the *Odyssey*, where Odysseus is praised for trying to hide his identity from Athena when he lands on the shores of Ithaca. The narrator says that Odysseus did not tell Athena the truth but chose his words carefully, using 'thoughts of great cunning' (13.255). Athena commends him for the tall tale he told her by describing him as cunning and knavish (13.291-5), and by comparing his ability to deceive to her own skill in deception.

By the fifth century, the Homeric glow seems to have faded, and Odysseus' deceptions were viewed, at least by some, as morally reprehensible. Clear indication of the reassessment is found in Pindar's references to the contest between Odysseus and Ajax for Achilles' arms after the defeat of Troy. In *Nemean* 7, Pindar declares that the only reason Odysseus won the prize was that Homer had led people astray by praising him beyond his worth. In *Nemean* 8, he says that Ajax, 'no speaker but brave hearted', was overtaken by oblivion, while the prize was given to 'cunning falsehood' (24-5) and the Greeks unjustly favoured Odysseus 'with secret votes' (26).

Euripides, too, treats Odysseus' deviousness and rhetorical skill as morally reprehensible. In his tragedy *Hecuba*, Euripides not only ascribes the decision to execute Hecuba's daughter Polyxena to Odysseus. He also has Odysseus justify the decision to Hecuba with self-righteous, self-satisfied arguments that comprehend neither the horror of the act nor the immensity of the mother's grief. In *Trojan Women*, he has the Herald tell Hecuba that Odysseus persuaded the Greeks to throw her grandson Astyanax from the walls of Troy so that no heir of Hector's would ever endanger them (722-4).

The Odysseus of Sophocles' *Philoctetes* is a complex character who does not readily fall into either of these moulds. Like Euripides' Odysseus, Sophocles' character too represents the pragmatic politician and smoothly justifies his deviousness. The text, however, neither extols his trickery, as Homer's epics did, nor judges it as harshly as Pindar and Euripides. As in his characterisation of Neoptolemus, so too in his depiction of Odysseus, Sophocles exploits the dual perspective on the trickster's character.

The contrasting perceptions of mythic figures teach us that, in and of itself, the bare plot of a myth does not tell us very much about the judgments that could have been made of it. They show that the events of the Philoctetes myth did not bind Sophocles or any of the other tragedians to a particular view of any of the characters in the story. The potential for multiple assessments of the same mythic figure was something that the playwrights could exploit to their own ends and interpretations. It is also likely that they could rely on their audiences, or at least the better educated among them, to bring their knowledge of perspectives that were not explicitly dramatised to bear on their understanding of their tragedies. This made the myths not only a rich repository of characters and stories, but also a source that enabled the playwrights to treat the issues that concerned them not in a narrow schematic way but with the complexity and lack of determinacy that are characteristic of life.

3

The Play

The synopsis given in this chapter is not a neutral rendering of the play's events. Like all writing, summarising entails choosing, ordering and arranging – acts which require interpreting the text. It is better to acknowledge the interpretation than to try to present the play's events as raw data. The interpretations are not elaborated, however, so as to minimise the inevitable overlap with subsequent chapters, where the same events and ideas are discussed in greater detail.

Prologos, 1-134

As pointed out in Chapter 1, the *prologos* conventionally paints the scene and provides the audience with whatever mytho-historical knowledge they require. In addition, *Philoctetes' prologos* introduces two of the play's three main personae, Odysseus and Neoptolemus, shows key elements of their personalities and dynamic, raises the chief dilemma with which the play deals, and establishes the ethical alternatives it explores.

Spoken in iambic trimeter, the metre of speech, the *prologos* opens with a twenty-five-line speech by Odysseus, the elder and dominant of the two. After introducing Neoptolemus to the audience as the son of Achilles and explaining how and why he had abandoned Philoctetes on Lemnos, Odysseus seeks simultaneously to gain Neoptolemus' co-operation and to assert his own commanding position. Creating a conspiratorial atmosphere, he cuts short his account of Philoctetes' abandonment as not very important (11-12), and explains that this is not the time for long conversations, since Philoctetes might overhear him and spoil his scheme. This warning creates dramatic tension and illustrates Odysseus' suspicious nature. In terms of characterisation, it shows Odysseus' manipulativeness as he tries to draw Neoptolemus into an alliance against a shared danger. At the same time, the older man asserts his dominance by informing Neoptolemus that 'your job is to help me' (15) and setting him on the errand to find Philoctetes' cave. He ends his speech with the lure of working together towards 'a joint enterprise' (25) – again flattering Neoptolemus with the prospect of partnership while firmly keeping the upper hand.

Neoptolemus responds as would be expected of a subordinate. Addressing Odysseus as his superior, 'Lord Odysseus' (26), he promptly sets out to look for the cave, which he soon finds. There follow ten lines (28-37) of *stichomythia* (a rapid exchange of single lines), in which Odysseus asks questions about Philoctetes' dwelling and Neoptolemus replies. Odysseus is concerned to make sure both that the cave Neoptolemus has found is Philoctetes' and that Philoctetes is not there (30). Once again, Odysseus' implication is that Philoctetes is dangerous, and the warning shows Odysseus' suspicious nature. The lines also show Odysseus as rather contemptuous of Philoctetes. In reply to Neoptolemus' description of the bed of leaves and poorly carved wooden cup in Philoctetes' cave, Odysseus comments, 'What you describe is his treasure' (37). The sarcasm is both obvious and callous. Odysseus is finally convinced that the cave belongs to Philoctetes only after Neoptolemus describes the pus-filled rags drying in the sun. Then he instructs Neoptolemus to send the scout to keep a lookout lest Philoctetes return and 'unexpectedly fall upon me' (46). Neoptolemus complies.

Neoptolemus also seems ready to comply when Odysseus, appealing to him to show his nobility, once again reminds him that 'you are here as my helper' (53). Dutifully, Neoptolemus asks, 'What do you command then?' (54). Once he hears the orders, however, he ceases to be so acquiescent.

The orders are to 'steal away Philoctetes' soul with your words' (55)[1] so as to get from him Heracles' unerring bow. Odysseus expands on this directive, instructing Neoptolemus to tell Philoctetes that he is Achilles' son, but nothing more of the truth. Instead, he is to tell him that he so hates the Greeks that he will not sail to fight alongside them in Troy and is sailing home to Scyros. His hatred he is to explain with a concocted story to the effect that the Greeks had refused to give him his father's arms when he asked for them, and had already given them to Odysseus. Put differently, Odysseus instructs Neoptolemos to deceive Philoctetes using a mixture of truth and falsehood, in which the truthful element (i.e. that Neoptolemus is Achilles' son) will lend credence to the false.

To motivate him, Odysseus informs Neoptolemus that the bow is essential for Neoptolemus to conquer Troy. This is a subtle distortion of the mythic prophecy, as familiar from other sources and as rendered later in the play (610-13), in which the bow was a requisite for the Greeks' conquering Troy and Philoctetes' participation was essential as well.[2] It is designed to appeal to Neoptolemus' desire for fame and glory and to obscure the fact that Neoptolemus will have to share these with Philoctetes. It also enables Odysseus to keep his options open, in case he cannot get Philoctetes to join the endeavour and must go it alone, as he will threaten in lines 1054-60.

Odysseus then explains why Neoptolemus, rather than himself, must carry out the deception: Philoctetes will not suspect Neoptolemus, who had not participated in his abandonment, but will promptly kill them both if he catches sight of himself. Odysseus ends his speech by acknowledging that such deception is inconsistent with Neoptolemus' noble nature, but assures him that time will prove that it was the right thing to do.

It is at this point that Neoptolemus balks. Unmoved by either the logic of Odysseus' explanation or the promised reward, he now rejects the scheme as inconsistent with the nobility of his nature and lineage. Offering to take Philoctetes 'by force' (90), he high-mindedly declares that he would rather err with honest action than triumph through treachery.

Neoptolemus' refusal shifts the dramatic tension from the threat supposedly posed by Philoctetes to the conflict between the two dramatis personae and the values they espouse. Then, in the ensuing *stichomythia*, Odysseus methodically breaks down Neoptolemus' resistance. From a dramatic perspective, there seems to be some reversal of roles, as Neoptolemus takes the lead, asking a series of questions: Are you telling me to lie? Why can't we use persuasion? Is Philoctetes so formidable that he can't be approached in a straightforward manner? Isn't it disgraceful to lie? But in fact Odysseus retains control. He convinces Neoptolemus that as long as Philoctetes keeps his bow, all attempts at force and persuasion will be futile. He spells out the advantages that Neoptolemus will gain from deceiving Philoctetes: the ability to capture Troy with Philoctetes' bow and a reputation for cleverness and valour. Having remained unmoved by the earlier lure of a reputation for duty, Neoptolemus now agrees to 'put aside all shame' and do Odysseus' bidding (120). The exchange shows Neoptolemus to be driven by the noble desire for fame and glory, as well as vacillating and easily corrupted. Odysseus' seduction of Neoptolemus foreshadows Neoptolemus' seduction of Philoctetes.

The *prologos* ends with Odysseus telling Neoptolemus that if the matter takes too long, he will send a scout disguised as a trader to facilitate it. How much Odysseus' purpose is to help Neoptolemus and how much it is to enforce his own will is an open question.

The dilemma raised in the *prologos* is how Philoctetes' bow

should be acquired, not *why* it is required, which is the question
dealt with in the myth. The remainder of the play is driven by
the ethical question of what the right way of getting the bow is.
Odysseus and Neoptolemus discuss this question and test all
three means suggested: trickery, force, and persuasion.[3]

The conflict between Odysseus and Neoptolemus is a conflict
of values, with the older man upholding the pragmatic use of
deception and the younger man proposing the two seemingly
more honest approaches of direct force and persuasion. It would
be erroneous, however, to presume a clear-cut ethical dicho-
tomy. Scheming may well be shameful and ignoble, as Odysseus
himself recognises. But is it any worse than Neoptolemus'
suggested recourse to force? The audience would probably recall
the savagery that this high-minded young man will exhibit in
Troy. In case they do not, Sophocles undercuts the heroic quality of his suggestion by having Neoptolemus support it with the
rather ugly observation that it should be easy for them to
overcome Philoctetes since he has only one good leg![4] The use of
persuasion, which Neoptolemus suggests next, may be morally
sounder, but the play will uphold Odysseus' argument that it is
not feasible. Philoctetes will not, in fact, be persuaded. Nor does
the play seem to support Neoptolemus' declared preference for
honest failure over success through treachery as a viable option. No one questions either the rightness of the Greeks'
ambition to defeat Troy nor the need to get the bow to do so.

The *prologos* thus poses a quandary to which there seems to
be no satisfactory solution.

Parodos (first choral song), 135-218

In most Greek tragedies, the *parodos,* the first choral song, is
an ode structured in strophic pairs, and sung and danced by the
Chorus alone. In *Philoctetes*, the Chorus sing and Neoptolemus
answers in recitative.

The Chorus consist of Neoptolemus' sailors.[5] They address him respectfully as their 'lord' and 'master' (135, 150) and look to him for leadership, as one endowed with the wisdom of a sceptre-bearing king (139-40). To some extent, their attitude, which contrasts strongly with that of Odysseus, is a function of their being Neoptolemus' social inferiors. Yet their address seems effusive and out of place, given Neoptolemus' youth and callowness (they themselves address him as 'child', 210) and the fact, which the audience would know, that in Homer neither he nor his father bore the high designation of a sceptre-bearing king. How much they are fawning and how much they are genuinely bewildered on the strange island, as they say they are, may be debated.

The Chorus offer to serve as willing helpers in whatever Neoptolemos wants to do. Nonetheless, they enunciate an independent view of Philoctetes, very different from both Odysseus' and Neoptolemus'. Calling him a 'sufferer' and expressing 'pity' for him, they paint a moving picture of him as isolated, ill and unjustly afflicted by the gods.

Their natural sympathy highlights Neoptolemus' callousness. Declaring that he is not surprised by Philoctetes' suffering, Neoptolemus offers a facile and solipsistic rationalisation of the hero's ordeal. Cruel Chryse was responsible for the snakebite, and his present troubles were visited on him by the gods so that he would not be able to fight in Troy until the ordained time. The implication is that the gods saw to it that Philoctetes was detained on Lemnos until Neoptolemus came of age and was ready to join him in the battle for Troy. Why they had to make Philoctetes so miserable in the meantime, Neoptolemus never considers. Whether Neoptolemus is so callous by nature or as a consequence of Odysseus' example is for the audience to decide.

3. The Play

First *epeisodion*, 219-675

This is the longest of the play's three *epeisodia*. It consists of four parts: Philoctetes' entrance and characterisation; Neoptolemus' successful 'theft' of Philoctetes' soul, the Trader's tale, and Neoptolemus' unexpected delay of his departure and temporary acquisition of Philoctetes' bow.

Philoctetes, whose entrance marks the beginning of the *epeisodion*, turns out to be very different from the threatening and suspicious character conjured up by Odysseus and the Chorus. He is welcoming, warm and interested in other people. He greets Neoptolemus and the Chorus enthusiastically (219) and addresses Neoptolemus affectionately as 'son' or 'child'. He is delighted that they are Greeks (233-4).

Along with these sociable qualities, the *epeisodion* shows Philoctetes to be excruciatingly lonely and miserable, yet resourceful, courageous and able to survive in the wild. Virtually the first thing he says about himself is that he is 'alone, desolate ... without a friend' (227-8). His great loneliness and longing for friendship make him particularly susceptible to the scheme to win his confidence. Between lines 254 and 316, he expatiates at length on his abandonment and hard life on the island. The speech provides little information that the audience has not already heard. It rather expands on what they know, to convey the impact of the abandonment on himself. Thus Odysseus had told us that he put Philoctetes ashore with his festering wound (7). Philoctetes tells that he was abandoned in his sleep with a few rags and some food, and relates his shock and sorrow when he woke up to find himself in pain and without anyone to help him. Similarly, Odysseus had conjectured that Philoctetes was out hunting birds. Philoctetes describes how his hunger drove him to hunting and how he shot the birds, fetched water, and cut wood dragging his bad leg, as well as how, making a fire by rubbing stones together, he managed to survive in the wild on

47

his own. Philoctetes' moving description highlights the callousness of his abandonment and the cruelty of the planned deception, wins the sympathy and respect of the audience and Chorus (317-18); and makes eminently comprehensible his hatred of Odysseus (46-7, 264-5, 315-16, 791-2, 984-5, 991-2, 1111-12, 1175, 1285-6) and his subsequent refusal to join the Greek venture in Troy (622-5, 994, 999-1000, 1001-2, 1040-4, 1197-203, 1275-7, 1367, 1392, 1400-1).

In the next part, Neoptolemus, following Odysseus' instructions, proceeds to gain Philoctetes' confidence by pretending to share his hatred of Odysseus and the Atreidae. Earlier in the *epeisodion*, he had already shown himself a highly competent liar and manipulator. He told Philoctetes that he was sailing home to Scyros (239-40) and he played unabashedly on Philoctetes' admiration and affection for Achilles (242-3). Now, after Philoctetes' long speech, he goes on to tell the story of how he was unjustly deprived of his father's arms (343-90), embellishing on the fabrication far beyond the bare outline Odysseus had suggested. The ever-loyal Chorus support his tale, though, logically, having sailed with him, they know that it cannot be true, since they did not sail to Sigeum.

With this story, Neoptolemus wins Philoctetes' trust and forges a bond based on their supposedly shared injury and hatred (403-5). Following some further conversation, Neoptolemus announces that he is going to his ship to set sail for Scyros, and Philoctetes implores him to take him along and drop him off at his home in Malis.

In the third part of the episode, the 'Trader'-*cum*-enforcer enters along with another sailor. The Trader, who was probably played by the same actor as played Odysseus (see Chapter 1), may be either the man Odysseus had said he would send to facilitate matters (126-34) or Odysseus himself in disguise.[6] The character's statements, like Neoptolemus' deception of Philoctetes, incorporate accurate information in a fabric of

falsehoods. His elaboration on the prophecy with the information that not only is Philoctetes' bow needed at Troy, but also
his presence, may be presumed to be accurate.[7] His assertion
that he has heard that Odysseus is on his way with Diomedes
to take Philoctetes to Troy, where he plans to put him on
display, is recognisably false. Odysseus is in Lemnos, not on the
way; and, however callous and coarse he may be, he is certainly
too clever unnecessarily to humiliate a man he will need to fight
for him. Neoptolemus plays along with the Trader, first solicit-
ing the story even though he knows it will be a fabrication and
then pretending to believe it.

In the fourth and last part of the *epeisodion*, Neoptolemus
announces that the wind has changed and that he must delay
his departure (639-40). Pressed by Philoctetes, he agrees to sail
anyway, but further stalls by suggesting that Philoctetes go to
his cave to fetch what he needs for the voyage. Then, hearing
that Philoctetes wants to get his arrows, he becomes interested
in his bow and asks to hold it. The two do not set sail. The
complication keeps the play from ending prematurely, as it
would have if Philoctetes had simply sailed with Neoptolemus
as planned.

The Trader's intervention has puzzled scholars,[8] yet is relevant for all three characters. The Trader's message seems to be
directed at Neoptolemus even more than at Philoctetes. The
information that Philoctetes' presence is required in Troy is
relayed out of Philoctetes' earshot and may be understood as a
veiled threat: that if Neoptolemus does not act with greater
alacrity and get Philoctetes on board, he will never be the great
hero he longs to be. Superficially, this threat seems to have the
desired effect. For the first time in his conversation with Philoctetes, Neoptolemus refers to the bow, though obliquely, as he
tells Philoctetes to fetch 'what matters most' to him from the
cave (645-6).

Yet, in sending the Trader just as Neoptolemus is about to

set sail with Philoctetes, Odysseus shows himself to be over-controlling and shortsighted. If anything, the Trader's visit delays the planned sailing. Moreover, the story the Trader tells about Odysseus' plans to put Philoctetes on display in Troy has the desired effect of frightening Philoctetes but will also prove self-defeating. Rather than making Philoctetes more malleable, the threat of being put on display at Troy (630) exacerbates his anxiety, precludes all possibility of co-operation, and contributes to his refusal to sail to Troy later in the play. May Sophocles be suggesting that Odysseus is too clever for his own good? May he be suggesting that it is the way of schemers to go too far and undo themselves (as Neoptolemus implies in lines 431-2)?

First *stasimon* (second choral song), 676-729

This is the only conventional choral ode in the play. Singing alone, the Chorus celebrate Neoptolemus' promise to take Philoctetes back home. Their being alone – that is, their not speaking to an inner audience that they would want to deceive – suggests that they believe him. It would also lead the audience to believe him as well. The Chorus' position is confusing, however, since they have been party to the deception of Philoctetes and, moreover, will soon advise Neoptolemus to filch Philoctetes' bow and make off for Troy with it (833-64). Is their pity real? It seems so, but can we be sure? Alternatively, is it perhaps an instrument of the Chorus' deceit?[9] That is, does their pity for Philoctetes further his deception – much as the truth that Neoptolemus is Achilles' son does? Or is it simply that they are unwilling to act on their pity? May it be that, like many of us, the Chorus gloss over moral contradictions and take whatever position suits them at the moment?

This inability to know people's minds is a recurrent motif in the play and part of its meaning. To bring home the point, and to emphasise the pernicious effects of deception, Sophocles, here and elsewhere in the play, places the audience in something of the same position of uncertainty as Philoctetes is vis-à-vis Neoptolemos.[10]

Second *epeisodion*, 730-826

This *epeisodion* is taken up with Philoctetes' sudden fit. It makes his agony palpable to the audience and places his suffering, helplessness and dependence on Neoptolemus at the centre of the play. Philoctetes, fearing that his groaning and paroxysms will make Neoptolemus unwilling to sail with him, alternately wishes for death and begs Neoptolemus not to leave him alone on the island. Neoptolemus repeatedly expresses concern and does what he can to help. He even offers to hold Philoctetes despite his repugnant smell.

Yet there is obvious irony in Neoptolemus promising not to set sail without Philoctetes. There is also dark premonition in Philoctetes' imploring 'Do not betray me out of fear' (757) and in his anxiety that Neoptolemus' prayer for a 'prosperous and speedy voyage to wherever the god thinks right' (780-1) may not be fulfilled (782). We may also note the ambiguity of the prayer. Where does the god think right – Malis or Troy?

The major action of this *epeisodion* is Philoctetes' handing over his bow to Neoptolemus for safekeeping. This, however, is only the first part of the ritual of delivery and return that we witnessed in the previous *epeisodion*. This *epeisodion* ends with Philoctetes fainting, covered with sweat, his head fallen back, and blood oozing from his wound, and with Neoptolemus directing the sailors to leave him in peace so that he may fall asleep.[11] We may wonder why he did not have the sailors take Philoctetes to the boat and thence to Troy. It would have been easy enough to do now that Philoctetes no longer has his magic bow. Is he moved by sympathy? Or does he simply feel no urgency to get Philoctetes on board and set sail? Or, may it be that he had really intended to take him home to Malis, and that his delay was a way of going back on his promise?

Kommos with Neoptolemus (lyric dialogue), 827-64

The Chorus and Neoptolemus sing a *kommos*, a lyric dialogue between the Chorus and a key character. It consists of two exchanges. In the first, the Chorus begin with a lullaby, calling on Sleep to bring Philoctetes release, and then go on to urge Neoptolemus to seize the moment. Neoptolemus rejects their urging, understanding it to mean that he take the bow and leave Philoctetes behind. His grounds are that the prophecy requires Philoctetes' presence for victory in Troy and also that taking the bow alone and 'to boast with falsehoods about actions incomplete' (842) would be disgraceful. The deception he terms shameful is evidently not of Philoctetes, but of the Greeks.

The *kommos* shows the Chorus ready to abandon Philoctetes even as they express pity for him, and Neoptolemus concerned with his honour. With Philoctetes asleep there is no need for deception: we can assume that both the Chorus and Neoptolemus say what they really feel.

Third *epeisodion*, 865-1080

This *epeisodion* is the most emotionally stormy in the play. It begins with Philoctetes' exhilaration when he wakes up to find that Neoptolemus has not forsaken him, and with Neoptolemus' joy in Philoctetes' recovery. Yet the mood shifts as soon as the two set out to the ship. The moment of decision has come. Neoptolemus can no longer continue to deceive Philoctetes and retain his friendship with him. Miserable and perplexed, he asks 'What should I to do next?' (895) Scheming contradicts his true nature (902-3) and he faces a knotty dilemma: he will be seen as a traitor whatever he does. If he takes pity on Philoctetes, he will betray Odysseus and the Greek army; if he continues with Odysseus' scheme, he will betray Philoctetes.

In an attempt to resolve the dilemma without choosing between two equally dishonourable courses, Neoptolemus tells Philoctetes their real destination. By this point however, Philoctetes is convinced that he will be taken to Troy only to be put on display and, unpersuaded, demands that Neoptolemus return his bow. Neoptolemus is forced to choose. He chooses his duty to Odysseus and the army (925-6) and refuses to return the bow.

Deprived of the instrument essential to his survival on the island, Philoctetes realises that he has been deceived. He alternately rages at Neoptolemus as unworthy of Achilles' heritage and beseeches him to return the bow, in keeping with the nobility of his nature (927-62, 967-8, 971-3). Moved by Philoctetes' despair, Neoptolemus once again feels pity for the crippled hero (965-6), and yet again, twice within five lines, asks what he should do (969, 974).

As he wavers, Odysseus suddenly enters and demands that Neoptolemus hand over the bow (974-5). Since Neoptolemus will give the bow to Philoctetes later on, it can be assumed that he does not comply.[12] What follows is an angry altercation (*agôn*) between Philoctetes and Odysseus. Philoctetes threatens to throw himself off a cliff to avoid being taken to Troy. Held back by two sailors, who seize him at Odysseus' orders, Philoctetes launches into a lengthy diatribe, lambasting Odysseus as the mastermind behind the deception and for his hypocrisy in being ready to sail with him now, vile odour and all, despite the fact that he is no less likely than before to disturb their libations.

Thwarted, and possibly stung as well, Odysseus changes tactics and tells Philoctetes that he can stay in Lemnos if he wants to. They have the bow in any case, he declares. Critics still debate whether Odysseus means what he says or is bluffing.[13] As we know by this point in the play, the prophecy requires Philoctetes' active participation in the fight for Troy, not only his bow. But it cannot be ruled out that Odysseus, ever resourceful and determined, will try to make do without him. In either case, Philoctetes takes the threat seriously. Facing death by starvation, he implores the Chorus not to leave him. Neoptolemus, taking pity though he knows Odysseus will disapprove, orders them to stay with Philoctetes while the boat is readied for sailing. His hope is that Philoctetes will change his mind in the interim.

Kommos with Philoctetes (lyric dialogue), 1081-217

This *kommos* consists of two strophic pairs, with each stanza divided between Philoctetes and the Chorus, who are at odds. Philoctetes, anticipating his inevitable starvation without his bow, yet again bewails his misery and yet again rages about the cruel deception perpetrated against him. That he does this in apostrophes to his cave and the birds he used to shoot rather than in a direct address to the Chorus is a measure of his alienation and withdrawal.

The Chorus respond by pointing an accusing finger: he has only himself to blame. Instead of acting reasonably, he chose the worse of the two alternatives (1095-100). The gods, not their deceit, they claim, is the cause of his misery. Nor is Odysseus to blame; he was only carrying out orders for the common good. In fact, it is in his own power to escape his deadly fate (1165-6). Philoctetes remains unmoved by the Chorus' admonitions. There is no indication that he even takes in what they say.

In the last strophic stanza, consisting of fifty-nine lines of statement and counterstatement, the Chorus tell Philoctetes that they went along with the scheme to take him to Troy because they believed that this was the best course (they do not say for whom). Philoctetes becomes even more enraged than before and tells them to leave him alone. However, as they are about to do so, he retracts and begs them to stay.

This *kommos* is the first time in the play that Philoctetes is explicitly presented as anything but a great and noble man who has been abominably treated and suffers unjustly. Though it is obviously self-serving, the Chorus' criticism of Philoctetes' stubborn unreason is not without sense. Where Philoctetes feels helpless and victimised, they point to his power to choose. Where he is in despair and on the verge of catastrophe, they offer life and hope.

Exodos, 1218-471

Neoptolemus finally breaks free of Odysseus' influence. Defying his erstwhile mentor, he declares his intention to return the 'shamefully' acquired (1234) bow, as he now terms it. His courage and moral transformation are evident as he sticks to his decision in the face of Odysseus' threats, first to attack him (Odysseus pulls out his sword) and then to bring the Greek army against him. After Odysseus exits, Neoptolemus calls Philoctetes from his cave so as to make good on his intentions. As he hands over the bow, Odysseus suddenly re-enters and forbids the act, but to no avail. Neoptolemus demonstrates his new-found maturity as he physically restrains Philoctetes, now in possession of the bow, from shooting Odysseus.

In contrast to Neoptolemus, Philoctetes does not change. Since he is now reconciled and grateful, Neoptolemus tries to persuade him to join the army at Troy. Framing the appeal as a personal request, he begins by chiding Philoctetes, much as the Chorus had, for inflicting his own wounds and for rejecting well meant advice. He also confirms the Chorus' assertion that the snakebite was the work of the gods, attributing it to Chryse. From here, he goes on to relate Helenus' prophecy that Philoctetes and he will take Troy with the help of Philoctetes' bow, and adds the information that Philoctetes' wound will not be healed until he comes to Troy. He ends his speech by holding up the fame that Philoctetes will win in helping to vanquish the city.

Philoctetes is as unmoved by Neoptolemus' arguments as Neoptolemus was by Odysseus'. Although he acknowledges that Neoptolemus 'gave me advice out of good will' (1351), he promptly goes on to explain why he cannot bring himself to join the men who had brought about his ruin. Arguing that Neoptolemus should not go to Troy either, he demands that the young man keep his promise and take him home. Following some wrangling, Neoptolemus agrees to do so.

The fact that he gave back the bow suggests that Neoptolemus is finally telling the truth. So does Heracles' entrance at this point. Heracles accomplishes what the human protagonists could not: Philoctetes will go to Troy of his own accord. The play ends with the crippled warrior bidding farewell to the deserted island.

*

Chapter 4 discusses the literary, intellectual, and political context in which the play was produced. Chapters 5, on Odysseus and Philoctetes, and Chapter 6, on Neoptolemus, both cover events up to Heracles' entrance, which is treated in Chapter 7.

4

Contexts

Like any enduring work of literature, Sophocles' *Philoctetes* can be approached from numerous perspectives. Some scholars have focused on the aesthetic aspects of the play, training their eyes on its dramatic structure and poetry.[1] Others have focused on what they see as its universal themes. More recently, critics have examined the play's background and contexts.[2] This chapter focuses on the play's adaptation of Homer and on the political and intellectual ambiance in which that adaptation was made.

The Homeric influence in ancient Greek tragedy has been widely recognised. Aeschylus' assertion that his tragedies were 'slices from the banquets of Homer' (Athenaeus 8.347e) is often quoted by scholars, and its application to Sophocles noted.[3] The Homeric influence was a natural product of the role and status of poetry in general and Homer in particular in fifth-century Athenian life. Throughout the fifth century, and even before, the study and practice of poetry was, along with gymnastics, an essential part of children's education. The *Iliad* and the *Odyssey* formed the core of the literary curriculum, and were staples of the cultural life of the ordinary citizen. Recitals from Homer accompanied by exposition were given by professional 'rhapsodists' who went from city to city and held public competitions among themselves. Homer was revered not only as the best of the poets but also an authority for knowledge, behaviour and morality.[4] Yet even against this background, the Homeric resonance in Sophocles' *Philoctetes* is striking, considering that

Philoctetes himself receives only brief mention in the *Iliad* and the *Odyssey*.[5]

Achilles, the great Homeric warrior, is a commanding presence in the play, even though he does not figure in any of the accounts of the myth that have come down to us. Sophocles brings Achilles into the play as Philoctetes' friend and model. Philoctetes is delighted to learn that Neoptolemus is Achilles' son (242-4), and trusts the young man largely on that account. He is startled and grieved to learn that Achilles has died (333-4, 336-8) and counts him as among the good and virtuous men whose lot it is to die in war when evil men survive (416-18, 426-30, cf. 435-7).

Philoctetes' affinity with Achilles extends to their values, character and behaviour.[6] Achilles chose a short life of fame and glory over a long, peaceful and unremembered existence. One of the first things that Philoctetes asks Neoptolemus is whether he has heard of him and whether people know of his deeds (249, 254-67). Achilles is an angry hero, whose 'wrath' (*Iliad* 1.1) unleashes the events of the *Iliad* and is mentioned repeatedly; so is Philoctetes. Achilles had removed himself from the battle for Troy after Agamemnon, the leader of the Greeks, had wronged him by appropriating his concubine. Philoctetes refuses to return to Troy after having been wronged by Odysseus. Achilles rejected the offer of compensation that Odysseus brought him from Agamemnon. Philoctetes is similarly adamant in rejecting Odysseus' offer of reconciliation.

In addition, Sophocles frames the conflict between Philoctetes and Odysseus in terms similar to the differences between Odysseus and Achilles in Homer. Homer's Achilles acted on personal motives. He absented himself from the battle when his honour was offended, and rejoined it not to further the common effort, but to avenge the killing of his friend Patroclus by the Trojan Hector. The Odysseus of the *Iliad* was a public person, always engaged and acting on behalf of Agamemnon and the other warriors. Achilles usually acted alone, reaching the height of his heroism in killing Hector in single combat.

In the *Philoctetes*, Odysseus is similarly the public man and Philoctetes the private. Odysseus invokes the protection of Athena of the Polis (134), Athens' guardian goddess, calls upon Neoptolemos to fulfil his duty to the Greeks, and threatens him with reprisals by the army if he does not. Philoctetes, the private man, welcomes Neoptolemus warmly and longs for human company, but when Neoptolemus disappoints him, he turns away from humanity and addresses his words to the elements (e.g. 986, 1081-2). His honour offended, he feels no more obligation than Achilles had to the Greek forces.

Homer's Achilles was the Greeks' best fighter; his Odysseus was their best speaker, better than Achilles in counsel. Achilles, proud of his fighting ability, freely acknowledged this difference (*Iliad* 18.105-6). Odysseus was equally proud of his special ability, boasting to Achilles that 'you are better than I am and mightier ... with the spear, but in counsel I greatly surpass you' (*Iliad* 19.217-19). Along similar lines, the Odysseus of the *Philoctetes* defines himself as a man of words (*logos*) as opposed to a man of action (*ergon*) and prides himself on his ability to make words work for him, as he tells Neoptolemus (96-9):

> ... I also had when young
> a sluggish tongue, but an active hand,
> now when I come forth to the proof, I see that tongue,
> not action, rules all things for mortals.

Philoctetes, in contrast, is the warrior whose active fighting in Troy is essential to victory.[7]

Homer's Odysseus, as we have seen, was a master of deception. His Achilles presented himself as a straight talker: 'Hateful as the gates of Hades in my eyes is the man who hides one thing in his mind and says another' (*Iliad* 9.312-13). Sophocles' Odysseus, like Homer's, is scheming, manipulative, and has no objections to deceit when it serves his purpose.[8] Lying is not wrong, he informs Neoptolemus, when it brings profit or advantage (107-13). Philoctetes is presented in the play as a truthful, principled individual who shares with his admired and valued friend a visceral hatred of lying and liars (403-58).

The Homeric dichotomies – between public and private motives and obligations, action and speech, truth and falsehood – are salient motifs in Sophocles' play and inform its characterisation and structure. Yet there is a fundamental difference. In the Homeric epics, the dichotomies are not quite as stark as the above account makes them seem. Achilles is not a dullard in counsel (e.g. *Iliad* 23.616-23), nor Odysseus all words and no fight (e.g. *Iliad* 10; 11.401-88). Their different excellences make them a bit critical of each other, but prowess on the battlefield and skill in counsel are both viewed as important, and most of the major figures in the epics are credited with both.[9] There is an overriding sense that each hero contributes his own special talents to the warrior club and that all their talents are valued and needed. This is not so in the *Philoctetes*. The play gives one set of values and traits to Philoctetes, the other to Odysseus, and brings in a third character, Neoptolemus, who must choose between them.

In fact, it may be suggested that Sophocles replaced Diomedes with Neoptolemus precisely to establish this situation. It is not only that Neoptolemus enables Sophocles to bring his famous father into the play. Sophocles needed a mythical figure whom he could present as struggling with the choices offered in the play, who could be pulled between Odysseus' demand that he deceive Philoctetes and Philoctetes' call to act in a manner becoming his noble birth. He needed a figure who could ask Odysseus, as his Neoptolemus does: 'You do not think then that it is shameful to tell lies?' (108), and ultimately decide that it is (120). Diomedes, Odysseus' partner in the espionage expedition against the Trojan forces in Book 10 of the *Iliad*, would not have filled the bill. In this episode, Diomedes selects Odysseus as his companion in espionage not only for his courage, but also, and perhaps more importantly, for his craftiness. Then, on his own initiative, he kills the Trojan spy that they find (Dolon) after Odysseus had promised not to harm him if he revealed the Trojans' secrets. On the other hand, none of the sources that have come down to us mentions either Neoptolemus' veracity or lack thereof. Sophocles was thus free to ascribe to him whatever characteristics he wished. The need to choose between contrasting alternatives sets Sophocles' Neoptolemus apart from his Homeric namesake and separates the *Philoctetes* from its Homeric foundations.[10] So do Neoptolemus' inner struggles as he wavers between one alternative and the other and the overwhelming sense of uncertainty that pervades the play.

This uncertainty in the *Philoctetes* is epitomised by the question 'What shall I do?'[11] This question is asked ten times in the course of the play, by all the human characters with the exception of Odysseus. Neoptolemus asks it five times (757, 895, 908, 969, 974), the Chorus twice (963, 1191), Philoctetes three times (949, 1063, 1350). The precise referent of the question varies with the speaker and the occasion. In general, it expresses Neoptolemus' and the Chorus' uncertainty about how to behave towards Philoctetes given the conflicting demands that are made of them, and Philoctetes' despair as he faces the hopeless choice between slow starvation on Lemnos and what he perceives as a humiliating return to Troy with his enemies. The multiple repetitions of the question highlight the uncertainties of the characters as they face dilemmas with no ideal solutions.

In short, we see Sophocles establishing Homeric underpinnings for his play and then deliberately departing from them. This is testimony to his skill and predilections as a dramatist.

61

The clash of characters, values and ideas is intellectually riveting, emotionally engaging, and enhances dramatic tension. The struggle of a character caught between alternatives heightens suspense. Indeed, the use of oppositions for dramatic purposes is a common Sophoclean technique.[12]

Beyond this, however, the attenuated antinomies and accompanying uncertainty reflect a very different sensibility from that of the Homeric epics, and illustrate the tendency, noted by scholars, of the fifth-century tragedians to adapt Homeric models to their own purposes and to the concerns of the age.[13] The remainder of this chapter will look at how certain features of fifth-century Athenian life, namely, the democratic polis, the teachings of the sophists, and the deteriorating political situation, may have contributed to differences in sensibility.

*

The simplest difference to account for is perhaps the conflict between personal and public, or civic, obligations in the *Philoctetes*. As scholars have pointed out, the relationship between the individual and the state is a recurrent and problematic issue in Athenian tragedy.[14] The conflict may be understood as a product of the democracy of the fifth-century Athenian *polis* (city-state).[15] This was a direct democracy which depended on the participation of all citizens, that is, of all free, Athenian-born men, in decision-making processes, as well as on their fulfilling a variety of civic duties, including military service. In the loose warrior fraternity of the Homeric world, the interests of the individual held pride of place. The hero fought for his own aggrandisement and glory. He came to the aid of his fellows less out of a sense of obligation than for personal honour and spoils. Thus Achilles could leave when he felt himself deprived of these.

As in any democracy, neither the state nor the individual was

clearly paramount. Athenians prided themselves on their democracy and viewed participation in the affairs of the city as
both a privilege and an obligation.[16] They understood the need
to work for the common good even to the point, at times, of
sacrificing their personal interests; to accept the decisions of
the majority even where they disagreed with them; and to obey
the laws and support state institutions. Yet, in contrast to
non-democratic states, where the interest of the state is clearly
paramount, there could be no hard and fast rule as to how to
choose when civic or public duty came into conflict with other
values (e.g. conscience, truthfulness) or obligations (e.g. to family, to the gods).[17] Choosing itself becomes the issue, as it does
in the *Philoctetes*.

The antinomies between talking and doing and between
truthfulness and deception may also owe something to the high
level of citizen participation in Athenian democracy. Athens
was a direct democracy, not a representative one. With the
exception of certain categories of lawbreakers, all citizens who
so wished were entitled to vote and participate in the debates
of the Assembly (the legislative body) and to serve in the
various governing bodies. Office holders were selected by lot, or
by popular vote, or by a combination of both. Men who wanted
to have a say in the affairs of the city thus had to be able to
address their fellow citizens and to convince them of the rightness of their views. Speaking and political activity were so
closely linked that politically active individuals were not only
termed politicians (*politeuomenoi*) or advisors (*symbouloi*), but
also orators (*rhêtores*) and speakers (*hoi legontai*).[18]

Under these circumstances, the functions and potential of
speech became salient issues in Athenian thought. On the one
hand, speech was valued as an indispensable tool of reasoning,
planning and decision-making, and understood as essential to
right action. Speaking ability, in this function, was closely
related to the all-important skill in 'counsel' in the Homeric

epics. At the same time, the Athenians were very wary of the corruptibility and corrupting power of speech in a society where all citizens could vote and men of undistinguished birth, character and mind could rise to leadership.[19]

The wariness of skilled speech was exacerbated by the activities of the sophists from the middle of the fifth century onwards. The word 'sophist' translates 'teacher of *sophia*' – itself variously translated as wisdom, cleverness or practical ability. In the fifth century, the term *sophist* referred to itinerant teachers who travelled from city to city providing instruction, for fees, in small circles and large public lectures. The sophists' instruction covered a variety of subjects, but its primary subject was rhetoric and public speaking, with particular attention to techniques of persuasion and argument. These were sought-after skills which gave those who possessed them advantages in the law-courts and in political life.[20]

The negative perception of sophistic rhetoric is evident in Aristophanes' burlesque, *Clouds*, produced at the Great Dionysia of 423. The plot concerns the newly rich rustic, Strepsiades, who, to evade his creditors in the law-courts, seeks instruction, first for himself and then for his son Pheidippides, from 'these people who teach, if one gives them money, to win whether one is arguing the right or the wrong' (98-9). 'These people' are the sophists. He wants to learn 'to split hairs, prattle narrowly about smoke, and meet a point with a counterpoint, pricking argument with counterargument' (320-1) – training which the Chorus leader tells him will enable him 'to pass more motions in the assembly' than anyone else (432). In the course of their instruction, Strepsiades and then Pheidippides are treated to a demonstration of how the Better Argument (personified as an elderly, traditional-minded gentleman and associated with the traditional moral education in virtue that the sophists were apparently challenging) is bested by the Worse Argument (personified as a young dandy and boasting a battery of sophistic skills). The Better Argument contends that he will win 'by presenting my just argument,' the Worse Argument that he will 'overthrow it with counterargument, for I absolutely deny the existence of justice' (900, 901-2). Strepsiades, too old to absorb the instruction, drops out of the programme, but Pheidippides completes the training. The upshot is that Pheidippides fulfils the prophecy of the chorus of clouds that Strepsiades will soon find 'a son who is formidable at arguing views opposite to what is right, so that he can beat anyone he meets, even if he argues what is totally base' (1313-19). At the end of the play, Pheidippides not only beats his father physically, but, applying his newly learned skills, succeeds in convincing him that it is just and right for sons to strike their fathers. Summing up, the Chorus describes the training as 'turning to evil deeds' (1455).

The dangers of eloquent speech were already alluded to in the *Iliad*, where the well spoken but base Thersites incited the troops against Agamemnon and had to be stopped by Odysseus' equally eloquent counterarguments (2.215-77). But this was a single incident in the world of the *Iliad*, where decision-making was the province of the well born warrior elite. In Athens' direct democracy, where rhetorical skill was a means of exerting influence and attaining advancement, the danger seems to have been considered much greater. Where Homer had alluded to the corrupting power of speech, Sophocles makes it a pivotal issue in the *Philoctetes*.

More fundamental than the specific dichotomies that are explored in the *Philoctetes* is the sense of uncertainty that pervades the play: three out of the four characters (assuming that the Chorus can be considered a character) find it difficult to choose between the options they face. They are painfully unsure about which values to adopt, which values to act on. Here, I would like to suggest that this sense of uncertainty may be seen, at least in part, as a product of both intellectual and political developments in Sophocles' Athens.

Intellectually, fifth-century Athens was a time of ferment. The sophists, like Socrates their contemporary, were developing a new way of thinking, and new approaches to the education of the young. The traditional style of education emphasised the development of morality through the teaching of poetry. In this approach, morality was based on tradition and accepted ideas. Socrates and the sophists challenged this approach, and its attendant moral assumptions, and insisted on the rational examination of beliefs previously taken for granted. Socrates focused on the nature of virtue. The sophists explored, among other issues, the nature of man and society and the relation between nature and custom or law.

Exactly what the sophists taught is shrouded in controversy. Only tiny fragments of their writings have survived; and what we know of their teachings comes mainly from a few summaries and the accounts of other Greek writers, especially Plato, who disliked them.[21] Moreover, they were independent philosophers and writers, not a coherent school or movement, so we cannot attribute to them a common set of doctrines. What is clear, however, is that, like the sophists' rhetorical teachings, efforts at systematic inquiry into matters of daily life and morality could have a disconcerting effect.

We may return to the *Clouds* to see something of the threat sensed in the sophists' intellectual approach. Situated in the Thinkery, as their academy is called, the sophists are presented not only as rhetoricians but also as the new teachers, who replaced the traditional education in morality with newfangled notions that undermine the moral foundations of society. Socrates is panned for his adoption of 'novel notions' (512-17). The Worse Argument boasts that 'I was the very first to think up the idea of arguing what is contrary to customs and justice' (1039-40). Among these 'customs' is belief in the gods. The clouds are the gods of the Thinkery, replacing the Olympic deities as the source of what happens on earth and as the objects of invocation and worship. But it is not only the sophists whom the play lambasts. The proponents of traditional education and values, as represented by the Better Argument, are shown not only as unable to hold their own against the sophists, but also as old, feeble, and intellectually incoherent.

In keeping with the conventions of Attic comedy, Aristophanes' depiction of the sophists is grossly exaggerated and distorted, though it may well reflect current stereotypes. What is important to the purpose here is the picture of profound moral confusion that the play presents and attributes to the sophists' rhetoric, rationalism and departure from tradition. The world of the *Clouds* is one where justice is scorned, the firm foundation of traditional religion replaced by air and vapour, and the most basic, universally accepted moral assumption – that children do not raise a hand to their parents – overturned. It is a world where the difference between right and wrong is not only blurred, but lost.

Sophocles would not have had to have attended the sophists' lectures or read their works to have felt the moral malaise depicted in the *Clouds*, or for this to have coloured the world of his *Philoctetes*. Nor need he have been familiar with the *Clouds* (though we may assume that he was) or have attributed the malaise to the sophists. The point is that the uncertainties that run through his *Philoctetes* and the difficulties his characters have in knowing which alternatives to choose might stem from and reflect a similar ambiance of moral breakdown.

This ambiance also seems to have owed something to the political developments of fifth-century Athens. During this period the regional power of Athens traces an arc of glorious rise and demoralising decline. Sophocles was born in about 496, when Athens' democracy was in its promising beginnings. In 479, when Sophocles was seventeen, the Athenian victory over

Persia in the Battle of Plataea put an end to the Persian threat to the Greek world, and ushered in almost half a century of security, enterprise, cultural and artistic achievement and maritime expansion. From the leading power in the Delian League, which it had organised for protection against Persia, Athens became the head of an expanding empire of tribute-paying city-states, which were associated with it in varying degrees of voluntariness. Its major politician, Pericles, was a man of extraordinary competence and leadership. Politically influential for almost a generation (till his death in 429) and the dominant figure in Athenian politics for thirteen of those years (443-429), he was responsible for much of Athens' cultural and political ascent from the mid-century onwards.

Things began to change with Athens' entry, under Pericles' urging, into war with Sparta and its allies in the Peloponnesian League. The Peloponnesian War, sparked by the Athenian growth and power which alarmed Sparta (Thucydides 1.23.6), lasted almost continuously from 431 to 404. Aside from brief intermissions, fighting went on in almost every part of the Greek world. At the beginning of the war, Athens had an unrivalled fleet and large financial reserves. It chalked up several naval victories. Things began to change with the outbreak of the plague in 430, during which around a quarter of Athens' population died of the disease, including about a third of its best troops and Pericles himself.

Pericles proved impossible to replace. As Thucydides describes them, the leaders who followed were less capable and more opportunistic individuals, who never commanded the respect he had (2.65). Although they pursued an aggressive war policy, the war did not go Athens' way. In the course of the decade, the Spartans were able to raise revolts in one city after another in the Athenian empire. By the end of the decade, Athens' politicians were split over whether to go on fighting or to pursue a policy of diplomacy and conciliation. As they fluctuated between the two in the decade that followed, the so-called allies continued to rebel, with Sparta's encouragement and assistance. In those instances where Sparta was not able to provide protection, the rebellions met with brutal Athenian reprisals.

In 413, Athens was brought to dire straits by its defeat in Sicily. Its army was routed at Syracuse, its fleet of over two hundred warships completely destroyed in a single battle. Its coffers were empty. Though Athens would start rebuilding its fleet and continue to fight, it was not to recover, either militarily or politically. The next few years saw political plotting (including some assassinations) and factional struggles driven more by opportunism than ideology. In 411, Athens' constitution was changed to restrict political rights to persons of means, and the rule of the polis was placed in the hands of a newly formed oligarchic Council of Four Hundred. The democracy was restored in 410. The Athenians' fortunes in their war against the Spartans varied in the next six years, but in 405 their navy was soundly defeated in the battle of Aegospotami. In 404, five years after Sophocles' *Philoctetes* was produced and two years after Sophocles died (406), Athens acknowledged defeat by Sparta.

The *Philoctetes* does not refer to any of these events. Nor, as scholars have concluded, can any of its dramatis personae be taken as stand-ins for any of the political figures of Sophocles' day.[22] We cannot even be sure when the play was written. The latest date is probably around 410, since plays had to be submitted for selection to the *archon eponymos* in the summer prior to the festival in which they were produced.

My claim is that the play's pervasive sense of uncertainty may owe something to the corrosive effects of the death of Pericles and the two decades of indecisive warfare and political strife that followed it. Thucydides (*c.* 460-400), the great historian of the Peloponnesian War, describes a deterioration of morals and morale in Athens beginning as early as the plague of 431, when obedience to the law, honesty and decency gave way to a live-for-the-moment ethos (Thucydides 2.52-3). Things did not get better as the war dragged on for decades following Pericles' death, without worthy leadership.

There must have been many people who wondered whether and how the debilitating war would come to an end. An honourable way out must have been difficult to see. There was the option of continuing to fight with depleted coffers, declining morale, and squabbling, uninspiring leaders, as Athens was doing when the *Philoctetes* was produced, or, conversely, dishonourable defeat by the Spartans. These were the kinds of choices that might well make thinking people cry out, 'What should I do?' The conundrum must have been all the worse when, under the influence of the sophists, the old values no longer provided a firm moral foundation or sure guide to action.

In 443-442, when he was in his fifties, Sophocles served as one of the chief financial officials (*Hellenotamiai*) of the Delian League (*IG* I.202.36) in which Athens' 'allies' were gathered. A close friend and political associate of Pericles, he took part with Pericles in the expedition to bring the rebellious Samos back into line (probably in 441-40; *FGrH* 324 Adrotion F 38) and served with him as a fellow general (*stratêgos*) – Athens' highest political office, with wide-ranging executive powers and great popular influence. Sophocles was the only one of the three tragedians to hold this office. When he was in his eighties, he was either a member of or advisor to the ten-man commission, the *probouloi*, that was appointed to deal with the state of emergency following Athens' defeat at Syracuse (Aristotle, *Rhetoric* 1419a25).[23] Given Sophocles' political involvement over a span of thirty years, it is only to be expected that he would have been deeply concerned with the social and political issues of his day and that his plays would reflect his concern.

In Chapter 1 it was noted that the conventions of ancient Greek tragedy made it eminently clear that the events they portrayed took place in another realm, beyond – and above – the mundane. The Homeric underpinnings of *Philoctetes* are entirely consistent with this aesthetic. Nevertheless, it may be assumed that the tragedies grew out of and reflected the concerns of the times in which they were written. Sophocles was an engaged poet, involved in the intellectual, political and religious life of fifth-century Athens. The *Philoctetes* is not a political play in the narrow sense of the term: it deals with universal issues that cross cultures and generations, and it does not take a clear stand on the issues of the day. The relations among the characters and the issues they grapple with can be appreciated without knowledge of the sophists, of Athenian democracy, or of the long and demoralising Peloponnesian War. However, knowledge of the intellectual and political milieu in which the play was written enhances our understanding of many of its details and probably brings us closer to the experience of Sophocles' audience.

5

Odysseus and Philoctetes

For many critics, the choice that faces Neoptolemus, and vicari-
ously the audience as well, is a simple one: between the pragmatic dishonesty that Odysseus shamelessly urges and the
high-minded principles of the put-upon Philoctetes. In this
reading of the play, Neoptolemus chooses either good or evil.[1]
This reading is an oversimplification.[2] It requires us to view
Odysseus as an entirely negative character and Philoctetes as
an entirely positive one, somewhat in the spirit of a medieval
morality play. The *Philoctetes* is of a different order, a work that
takes into account the complexities both of human nature and
of external reality. The choice is difficult because the question
the play explores is not what is right in abstract terms, but
what is the right course of action under circumstances where
the moral and the practical are at odds or where different moral
goods collide. These complexities are conveyed through the
ambiguous portrayals of Odysseus and Philoctetes.

Odysseus

Of the two characters, Odysseus comes across as the less attrac-
tive. Already in the *prologos*, he shows himself to be callous,
suspicious and manipulative (see Chapter 3). In his opening
speech, aimed at winning Neoptolemus' co-operation in his
scheme to trick Philoctetes out of his bow, he is also exposed as
trying to justify himself by any means available. Thus he
justifies having marooned the injured Philoctetes on Lemnos

with the two-part claim that he was ordered to do so by 'those in command' and that Philoctetes' cries at their religious celebrations haunted the camp and brought bad luck. His avoidance of naming 'those in command' (though the audience knows they are Agamemnon and Menelaos) makes him sound as if he is hiding behind the orders of his superiors while shielding them to boot. On he other hand, his presentation of religious grounds for abandoning Philoctetes implies that he supported the action as the correct thing to do, and raises the question why he bothered to invoke authority.

The ancient Athenians were probably no more inclined than we are to accept following orders as adequate grounds for morally questionable behaviour. Something of their attitude may be gleaned from Pericles' funeral oration for the Athenian soldiers fallen in the first year of the Peloponnesian War. In this paean to Athens, Pericles describes Athenians as law abiding out of respect and as giving 'obedience to those in authority and to the laws, especially those established to help people who have been wronged and those which, though unwritten, all agree bring shame on the transgressors' (Thuc. 2.37). He goes on to declare that 'we Athenians either consider or discuss our affairs properly' (2.40). Albeit idealised, and the ideal somewhat faded by the end of the century, this description is of a society where obedience is conditioned on the agreed morality of the law and where individuals, whether singly or jointly, are responsible for decisions on state policy. In similar vein, in the Ephebic oath sworn upon the completion of military training, the young soldiers (*ephebes*) swore to obey their commanders and the rulers of the country – so long as their orders were 'just'.[3]

The play depicts Odysseus as a sleazy politician tainted by sophistic values and rhetoric.[4] In *Clouds*, the Chorus leader promises the aspiring Strepsiades that he will be truly blessed if, 'as befits a clever man, you consider this the very best thing: to win in action, in counsel, and in waging war with your tongue' (418-19), while Strepsiades anticipates 'twisting law-suits to my own advantage' (434) when he acquires the sophists' skills. The sophists' reputed valuation of cleverness and their vocabulary of victory and advantage colour all Odysseus' deal-ings with Neoptolemus and Philoctetes. Odysseus assures Neoptolemus that he will be called 'clever' if he deceives Philo-ctetes (119), and reproaches him with not being clever when he is about to return Philoctetes' bow. He tells him that it is wrong to hesitate 'when you do something for profit' (111), urges him to 'get whatever is useful' from the concocted tale that the Trader will tell (131), and declares that 'it is delicious to lay hold of the riches of victory' (81), that 'it is in my nature always to desire victory' (1052).

Like the sophists, too, Odysseus is a self-proclaimed man of words (96-9) who twists logic and language to his own purpose. This was evident already in his specious justifications for aban-doning Philoctetes on Lemnos. We see it again in the moral and linguistic confusion of lines 81-5, where he promises Neoptole-mus that the 'justness' of their act will become apparent once they trick Philoctetes out of his bow, and then pledges that if Neoptolemus gives himself over to him 'shamelessly' for a single hour he will in exchange 'be called the most pious of mortals for the rest of time'. The first statement presents deception as a moral act; the second confounds justice with the reputation for it and implies that this reputation is best obtained by reprehen-sible conduct. A similar moral and verbal muddling is evident in Odysseus' description of himself as the quintessential man of the moment, who acts as expediency requires.[5] Whenever there is need for someone who is manipulative and dishonest, Odys-seus practically boasts (1049-51):

> ... I am such a man;
> and wherever there is a test of just and good men,
> you will find none more pious than I.

His yoking of piety and deceit makes the same nonsense of language and morality as his yoking of shamelessness and justice.

The play also depicts Odysseus as an unheroic character. He brings Neoptolemus along on his mission because he is afraid that Philoctetes will attack him (70-6). He insists on taking Philoctetes by guile rather than by force or persuasion because there is no evading Philoctetes' arrows (105). Trying to keep Neoptolemus from returning Philoctetes' bow, he makes as if to strike him with his sword (1254-5); but, when Neoptolemus proves unafraid, retreats and threatens him with the army instead (1255-6, 1257-8, cf. 1243).[6]

By drawing Odysseus as an ageing politician who has lost his youthful idealism and by showing his antiheroic quality as inseparable from his crudeness, insensitivity and lack of courage, the play demonstrates how little there is to admire in the ethos of deception. Yet the play also allows for a more positive reading of Odysseus' character: as prescient, practical and motivated as much by common interests as personal ones.[7] Odysseus' concern that Philoctetes will kill him if he catches sight of him (70-4), his prediction that Philoctetes will not be persuaded to go to Troy, and his insistence that the journey to Troy is the will of the gods (990) are all borne out by the events of the play. His presence of mind is shown as he moves rapidly to prevent Philoctetes from committing suicide. Moreover, however questionable his means, Odysseus is nowhere presented as corrupt or self-serving.[8] On the contrary, his aims are clearly consistent with the interests of his fellows and the plans of the gods.

Nor should Odysseus' arguments for expediency be viewed as necessarily reprehensible. Thucydides' *History of the Peloponnesian War* shows the language of expediency to be a recurrent feature of fifth-century Athens' contemporary political discourse. In the Mytilenian debate, which concerns the proper

Athenian response to the Mytilenian revolt of 428 (3.35-48), both speakers argue that the course of action they advise is in Athens' interest. The politician Cleon urges that executing all the adult males of the city and enslaving the women and children is both just and expedient (3.40). His opponent, Diodotus, counters that even if they all deserved punishment, executing only those who actively participated in the rebellion is to be preferred as the more beneficial course of action (3.44, 47). Similarly, in the Melian Dialogue of 416 (5.84-113), both the Athenian envoys who demanded that the Melians give up the island's neutrality and submit to Athens' superior power and the Melian magistrates who rejected the demand present their position as mutually beneficial. In Sophocles' play, even Philoctetes seems to understand the importance of 'profit'. He informs Neoptolemus that the island has so few visitors because it offers no place where sailors can 'trade for gain or find hospitality' (303). Later on, he offers Neoptolemus a number of rewards (the appreciation of his father Poeas, the opportunity to take vengeance against Odysseus for stealing Achilles' arms, and the chance to prove himself superior to Odysseus and his lot) for not joining the expedition against Troy.

Philoctetes

Even before Philoctetes makes his appearance, Odysseus' sleaziness, callousness and contempt predispose one towards the abandoned warrior by way of contrast, while the Chorus' pity and empathic depiction of his pain, loneliness and sickness (169-90) and his own agonised cry from the *parodos* (201-9) elicit sympathy for him as a wronged and suffering hero.

Philoctetes' conduct in the first *epeisodion* reinforces this sympathy and, moreover, elicits admiration and respect. The enthusiastic welcome he gives Neoptolemus and the Chorus and his openness, warmth and curiosity about them mark him as a friendly, sociable individual, far from the suspicious and fearsome bugaboo that Odysseus had conjured up. His account of how he survived by shooting doves on the wing; crawling, dragging his injured foot to get close to them; cutting wood, and rubbing stones together to make a fire against the cold, all this shows him to be courageous and resourceful. The pathos and humility with which he begs Neoptolemus to take him home (468-506), his awareness that the stench of his festering wound may cause 'discomfort' (473) aboard the ship, and his readiness to stay wherever he will cause least offence (483) point to his sensitivity and consideration for others.

Our sympathy is with Philoctetes as he describes his loneliness and abandonment, as we watch him in the agony of his spasm, and as we hear his anxiety that Neoptolemus may not take him home because of his loud groans and noxious odour. We are indignant as we watch Neoptolemus prey on his trust and his longing for human company to deceive him with the concocted story of the stolen arms. We are distressed by the misplaced trust with which he gives Neoptolemus his bow for safekeeping and are moved by his gratitude, so ironic under the circumstances, when he wakes up after his spasm and finds that Neoptolemus has not abandoned him. Sophocles so builds our sympathy for Philoctetes that we not only understand his hatred of Odysseus and refusal to join his erstwhile friends at Troy, but also accept these positions emotionally.

For some two-thirds of the play, Sophocles makes it easy to take Philoctetes as an epitome of rectitude and to overlook his less admirable qualities.[9] For example, when Neoptolemus deceives Philoctetes with the story of the arms, it probably does not occur to us that Philoctetes may have made himself an easy mark by his hatred for Odysseus and his eagerness to hear tales about his enemy, even though we soon hear him cursing Odysseus and wishing his death (416-18, 429-30). Similarly, his fierce invective and imprecations after Neoptolemus refuses to

return his bow (927-62) come across as the natural and understandable response of a man who has been betrayed by someone
he trusted and who now faces the grim prospect of death by
starvation, and we probably do not grasp the destructive consequences of his rage.

Beginning in the middle of the third *epeisodion* (976), however, Sophocles introduces a critical perspective. At the same
time as he maintains the audience's sympathy for Philoctetes,
he frames the hero's encounters with the other participants so
as to raise questions about his character and conduct.

With Odysseus: The shift in perspective begins when Philoctetes encounters Odysseus face-to-face. In response to Odysseus' threat to take him to Troy by force, Philoctetes first tries
to kill himself by jumping off a high pinnacle and then, when
this effort is foiled, unleashes a furious tirade filled with wishes
for Odysseus' death and expressions of self-pity.[10] Both responses may be seen from dual perspectives.

Philoctetes' attempt to kill himself may be seen as a moving
demonstration of the desperation of a noble mind driven to
avoid shame by the only means he believes he has. Watching
him lurch towards the rock, as the scene may have been staged,
would make that desperation all the more palpable. Yet the
ancient Greek attitude towards suicide was ambivalent.[11] Suicide was met with understanding as a response that warriors
might make to shame and dishonour, but was not considered
manly or noble. Honourable death for a man was death in
battle, not death by his own hands.

Philoctetes unleashes his tirade (1004-44) as he is being
restrained by Odysseus' sailors, who have been ordered to
prevent him from killing himself. As he is held against his will,
humiliated and helpless to do anything but lash out verbally,
his harangue seems to project an inner power and strength. His
critique of Odysseus' tawdry and hypocritical behaviour – en-
trapping himself by using Neoptolemus as a screen, exploiting

Neoptolemus' youth and obedience, and the hypocrisy of the excuses Odysseus made for marooning him on Lemnos – is cogent and well articulated, if not entirely accurate. Moreover, Sophocles' audience is likely to have been sympathetic to Philoctetes' apprehensions that he will be tied up and taken to Troy by force and that, once there, Odysseus and the Atreids will humiliate and mock him. The freedom and honour, which Philoctetes fears losing, were core attributes of ancient Athenian manhood and of great concern not only to the Homeric warrior, but also to the Greek male of Sophocles' day.[12] Indeed, the play has shown Philoctetes' apprehensions to be well grounded: in the Trader's warning that Odysseus intends to put him on display in Troy (616), in Odysseus' threat to take him to Troy by force (983), and in the humiliation of having been thrown out of the Achaean company 'dishonoured' (1028) ten years earlier.

At the same time, the invective in the speech reaches a saturation point. Within forty-one lines, Philoctetes hopes that Odysseus will perish and die a miserable death, says that he has prayed for his death, predicts that he will perish, and asks the gods to punish the Achaeans for what they did to him. This is not the first time that we hear Philoctetes cursing, wishing Odysseus dead (e.g. 416-18, 429-30, 961), or praying for his enemies' requital (315-16, 1369). There is only so much cursing, however, that one can uncritically accept as a manifestation of the curser's pain. We begin to sense the destructiveness of Philoctetes' fury, which spares neither others nor himself, and whose ultimate expression seems to be a rush towards death.

Our reservations are strengthened by the self-pity that infuses the outpouring. Philoctetes' depiction of abandonment, friendless, deserted, citiless and a corpse among the living, is similar to earlier self-portrayals (e.g. 254-99). Yet while those had been aimed at providing information and raised pity incidentally, repetition of the same information here gives the impression that Philoctetes is harping on the past and holding on to his sense of victimisation. This impression is reinforced by the contrast he draws between Odysseus' undeserved happiness and his own troubles.

By the end of Philoctetes' tirade, it is hard not to agree with the Chorus' judgment: 'Bitter is the stranger and bitter his speech, that does not yield before his troubles' (1045-6).

With the Chorus: Sophocles similarly creates a double perspective in Philoctetes' *kommos* with the Chorus. In the first two strophic pairs (1081-162), Philoctetes strikes a note of pathos, as he repeatedly anticipates a lonely death by starvation, bewails his isolation when the Greeks leave, bemoans his helplessness, and decries the deception that reduced him to his wretched condition. His apostrophes to his cave, to the birds and the beasts, and to his beloved bow show him turning away from the human beings who have betrayed him and seeking succour in inanimate objects and the world of nature. His vision of Odysseus sitting on the shore and mocking him while brandishing his bow conveys his deep anguish. His image of the birds of prey and the wild beasts he had previously hunted coming to take their revenge movingly conveys his helplessness and the grimness of his future. The pathos is intensified by the fact that the lines are sung.

After each stanza, however, the pathos is cut short by a choral admonition. He has chosen his grievous situation, the Chorus tell him. Had he shown good sense, he could have made a different choice. He came to his impasse not through deceit, but through 'fate from the gods'. They caution him to direct his hatred elsewhere and hope that he will not reject their friendship. They tell him that a man should 'not thrust out a hateful tongue' that 'gives pain'. They point out that Odysseus followed orders and did a service to his friends. And, finally, they beg him to regard their friendship and tell him that it is in his power to 'escape this deadly fate' (1166).

The Chorus' admonitions are clearly self-serving. Their reproaches justify the Chorus' complicity in Neoptolemus' trickery, in their confirmation of Neoptolemus' tall tale of the appropriation of his father's armour (391-402) and their advice that Neoptolemus should steal Philoctetes' bow while he is asleep (833-8, 843-64).[13] They deny the pain caused Philoctetes by Odysseus' deceit and their own, justifying the deceit with the dubious excuse that Odysseus was following orders. Moreover, given their previous behaviour, the friendship they ask Philoctetes not to reject must be suspect. All of this makes it impossible for the Chorus to serve as an authoritative voice in the play, a function served by the choruses of many of the Greek tragedies that have come down to us.[14]

Nonetheless, can we deny that Philoctetes has chosen the *impasse* in which he finds himself or that he could have chosen differently? After having heard his harangue against Odysseus, might we not agree that it is better to curb a hate-filled tongue? Would we dispute their claim that Philoctetes can still avoid the 'deadly fate' he has chosen? And would we not accept as apt and genuine their concluding observation that this fate 'feeds pitifully' on him 'and whoever lives with it cannot understand how to support its countless burdens' (1167-8)?[15]

In the *epode* (1169-217), Philoctetes' behaviour becomes increasingly distraught, irrational and rigid. Demanding to know why they destroyed him, Philoctetes replies to the Chorus as one who has grasped nothing at all of what they have said. When the Chorus explain that they believe that taking him to Troy is 'best', he orders them to leave him; then, as they are about to depart, he begs them to stay. Yet, even as they stay, he adamantly refuses to be guided by them and, instead, curses Ilion and begs them for a sword with which to 'cut off my head and every limb' (1207). 'My mind is on killing, killing', he tells them; and when they ask him why, he replies 'To look for my father … in Hades' (1210).

Philoctetes' manner of speaking in these lines sounds like

81

the verbal equivalent of writhing in agony and shows him to be 'distraught by a storm of grief' (1194-5). Yet the lines also show him yet again turning away from succour – after all, the Chorus do stay – and choosing death over any other solution. If we had earlier wondered whether suicide was perhaps not the right way of resolving the dilemma, by the end of the *kommos* we are increasingly suspicious of it as the choice of a hate-filled irrational mind.

With Neoptolemus: A similar tension between emotional sympathy and intellectual distance is created in the scene where Philoctetes rejects Neoptolemus' last plea that he fight with the Greek army at Troy. Neoptolemus has returned the bow, so the sincerity of his friendship, unlike that of the Chorus, is not in question. He bolsters his plea with the inducements of healing and fame. If Philoctetes comes willingly, Neoptolemus promises, his wound will be healed by the great physician Asclepius and he will 'win the highest fame' (1343-7). The audience have heard Philoctetes repeatedly decry his lameness and sickness, the pain and stench of his wound, and the many troubles it has caused him. They have also heard the value he places on his personal fame. One of his first questions to Neoptolemus was whether he had ever heard of him (251-2); and when Neoptolemus answered in the negative, he described himself as 'hateful to the gods, since no report of my circumstances has reached home or any place in Greece!' (254-6). In other words, going to Troy will bring Philoctetes precisely what he most wants.

The opening words of Philoctetes' reply, 'O hateful life, why do you still keep me alive above ground, nor release me to go to Hades?' (1348-9), are thus rather jarring. We have become accustomed to hearing Philoctetes wish for death. Now, however, he would appear to have within his grasp much of what he wants: his bow and the potency it gives him; the proven friendship of Achilles' son; and the prospect of healing, fame and the community of men after his long illness, obscurity and isolation. How are we to view his refusal? As the rejection of a bribe and an act of noble self-sacrifice in the name of a higher value? As an admirable preference for honour at any price, even death? Or are we to see it as perverse, self-defeating, and destructive?

His speech shows a man who is internally divided yet unable to give up his rancour. Philoctetes recognises that Neoptolemus' counsel is given out of good will (1350-1), but declares that he cannot follow it.[16] In a succession of questions, each only a slight variant on the one before, he asks how he can yield after what Odysseus has done to him (1352-7). The repetitiveness of the questions conveys his stuckness. He claims that his refusal is motivated not by past events, but by the sufferings he foresees at the hands of the Argives in the future. This is an understandable apprehension. But how much credence can we give it? Is there anything in the text, before or after, that even hints that Philoctetes no longer bears an all-consuming grudge?

Neoptolemus had couched his plea as a personal request (1315-17). His hope seems to be that now that he has proved his friendship, Philoctetes will reciprocate in kind. Instead, Philoctetes insists that Neoptolemus do as he himself wants. He begins, midway in his speech, by asking how Neoptolemus can go to Troy to fight on the side of men who robbed him of his father's 'gift of honour' (1364-5) and then have the nerve to urge him, Philoctetes, to join him. Then he demands that Neoptolemus make good on his earlier promise to take him home to Malis and stay in his own home in Scyros, so as to deny the Argives his assistance.

Philoctetes frames his demands as the moral course. A noble person, he implies, does not overlook insults; an honourable person keeps his word. We may wonder, however, whether he is not a bit too ready to use Neoptolemus for his own ends, much as Odysseus had done. This suspicion is strengthened as their discourse unfolds in thirteen lines of rapid *stichomythia* until

Philoctetes gets his way. In these lines, which quicken the pace and heighten the tension after the two long speeches, Philoctetes holds Neoptolemus to his promise, while ignoring, dismissing or summarily rebutting every one of the points that Neoptolemus makes. Philoctetes' importunities are filled with emotional blackmail, as he insists that Neoptolemus will destroy him by taking him to Troy and demands that Neoptolemus yet further prove his friendship for him by violating his commitments to Odysseus and the Atreids. Since, at this point in the play, Neoptolemus feels bound by his friendship and by Philoctetes' strict code of honour, he has no way of resisting. He cannot even bring himself to say that he had never meant to take Philoctetes to Malis. Then, after Neoptolemus gives in, because he sees no way not to, Philoctetes remains undeterred by the dire consequences Neoptolemus will suffer. He simply tells Neoptolemus not to worry about the Achaeans' rebukes, and promises to help him out with the inescapable arrows if they come to ravage his country.

Friendship was a central value in ancient Greek culture. A man was expected to care for and protect his friends, to help them materially, and even to sacrifice his own interests for them.[17] Neoptolemus proves his friendship. Philoctetes does not. His lapse is particularly sad and ironic in light of his repeated complaints about his loneliness and his declared friendship for Neoptolemus' father.

*

In his characterisation of Odysseus and Philoctetes, Sophocles brings the audience's judgment to bear on their own emotional responses. The antipathy that Odysseus arouses by his insensitivity and mendacity is tempered, though by no means eradicated, as he proves himself correct in crucial respects and as the consequences of Philoctetes' all-consuming hatred unfold. The sympathy that Philoctetes never ceases to garner is tempered by reservations about the destructiveness of his hatred and its power to blind him to all else, including the well-being of his friend.

The play shows the limitations both of Odysseus' guile and ethos of expediency and of Philoctetes' cleaving to Achillean honour and principle.

Odysseus' readiness to resort to deception when it suits his ends makes it impossible to know when he is and is not telling the truth. The requirements of the prophecy, which seems to make the defeat of Troy contingent on Philoctetes' willing participation in the fighting, suggest that Odysseus may never have had any intention of taking Philoctetes to Troy by force; that he was telling the truth when he assured Philoctetes that he would not be a slave in Troy, but a fighter, 'equal to the best men' (997), and that he was once again bluffing when he declared that, now that he has Heracles' bow, he no longer needs Philoctetes (1055-62),[18] as well as when he threatened to leave Philoctetes to starve on Lemnos. Yet, based on his experience, Philoctetes had every reason both to believe Odysseus' threats and to disbelieve that he would be well treated in Troy. As for the audience, whatever they may assume from their knowledge of the myth, they really have no way, from the play itself, of being certain of Odysseus' intentions or of anything he says. Such, the play suggests, are the uncertainties and misapprehensions bred by deception.

Indeed, the uncertainty and inability to trust bred by his double deception, by Odysseus and then by Neoptolemus, fuel much of Philoctetes' fury and intransigence. One critic contends that if Neoptolemos had not deceived him, Philoctetes would have been more amenable to persuasion.[19] Whether or not this is so is open to debate, in view of Philoctetes' long years of suffering and his abiding hatred of the men who abandoned him. However, Odysseus' utilitarianism and unreliability certainly contribute to Philoctetes' refusal to believe his assertion that the gods desire his presence in Troy (989-90) and Neoptolemus' subsequent rendition of the prophecy (1326-42). Thus, even as the play comes short of teaching that trickery is never to be considered or employed, it shows Odysseus' policy of guile rebounding on itself.

Likewise, in depicting Philoctetes, the play seems to point up the limitations of the Achillean values he espouses. Achilles is a scantily sketched figure in the play. Odysseus calls him the mightiest father among the Greeks (3) and noble (96); Philoctetes calls him the best of the Greeks and 'a father most dear to me' (242, cf. 1284, 1313). Neoptolemus tells us that it was not Achilles' nature to engage in 'evil scheming' (89), and his story of Odysseus depriving him of Achilles' arms reminds the audience that Achilles was a consummate warrior. These vague and unnuanced references are consistent with the post-Homeric representation of Achilles as a martial hero exemplifying his aristocratic heritage and a man of truth and action.[20]

Sophocles' development of Philoctetes' association with Achilles makes him a great hero in the ancient tradition, but also highlights the high price to be paid in suffering for his uncompromising insistence on righteousness. Sophocles, unlike Euripides, refrains from directly challenging the contemporary image of Achilles.[21] His presentation of Philoctetes, however, harks back to the more complex depiction of Achilles in the *Iliad* in a way that recalls the reservations Homer had already expressed about Achilles' conduct and the values he embodied. The *Iliad*, as the better part of the play's audience would have remembered, begins with a call to the Muse to 'sing the wrath ... of Peleus' son, of Achilles, the devastating wrath that brought the Achaeans measureless pain' (1.1-2). These lines emphasise the suffering Achilles' wrath caused his own people. Sophocles similarly emphasises the devastating implications of Philoctetes' fury: for his enemies, himself, and his friend. In

5. Odysseus and Philoctetes

Book 9 of the *Iliad*, Achilles rejects the gift offerings brought by
the Argive delegation to compensate him for the dishonour he
suffered at the hands of Agamemnon and to try to bring him
back to the battlefield. Homer shows how his refusal to compro-
mise his honour led to the death of his dear friend Patroclus,
who was killed when he went out to fight in Achilles' stead.
Philoctetes' rejection of Neoptolemus' inducements (fame and
healing) to go to Troy and his insistence that he take him home
to Malis puts Neoptolemus in a moral and emotional quandary,
jeopardising his standing with the Atreids and the safety of his
homeland. By the end, it is hard not to ask whether adherence
to principles, as Philoctetes embodies it, is always preferable to
the expediency preached and practised by Odysseus.

Through his characterisation of Odysseus and Philoctetes,
Sophocles shows the enormous complexity of the choices facing
Neoptolemus, as Odysseus demands that he fulfil his obligations to the community and Philoctetes that he fulfil his
personal obligations to himself. He shows Odysseus' dishonesty
mobilised to serve the aims of the community and the will of the
gods, but also how that dishonesty corrodes the trust on which
social relationships are based. He shows Philoctetes as morally
superior, but shows his integrity as inseparable from his rage,
running counter to the divine plan, dooming him to isolation,
and leading to death and destruction.

6

Neoptolemus

Sophocles treats Neoptolemus' choice on two planes, ideological and personal. On the first, he shows Neoptolemus grappling with the moral and social values represented by Philoctetes and Odysseus. These can be conceptualised as the principled adherence to truth whatever the cost versus the use of deception when the end seems to require it, and at the same time as the adherence to personal principles and obligations versus the fulfilment of civic responsibilities. On the second plane, he shows Neoptolemus working out the issues in a quasi-familial situation.[1]

Philoctetes is one of only a few extant tragedies whose action does not revolve around a family conflict (e.g. *Ajax, Trojan Women*) and the only one that has no female characters. The myth of Philoctetes' abandonment and recall to Troy involves relations among men who belong to the same warrior fraternity but are not related by blood. On the basis of the myth, Sophocles treats issues of trust, betrayal, and the obligations men have towards one another. He does, however, create a quasi-family situation by depicting Neoptolemus as a fatherless young man coming of age.[2] That is, he shows Neoptolemus as a late adolescent batted between the competing claims of Odysseus, who would be his teacher, and Philoctetes, who assumes a paternal role. Achilles' son makes his choices as he strives to define his identity within the changing relationships between young men and their elders.[3] This chapter traces his struggle, waged both externally (vis-à-vis Odysseus and Philoctetes) and internally, for self-definition.[4]

Nomos and *physis*: nature and nurture, teacher and father

Sophocles frames Neoptolemus' struggle, and the competition between Odysseus and Philoctetes, within the fifth-century debate about the relationship between nature and nurture: *physis* and *nomos*. *Physis* referred to a person's nature, which was presumably inherited. *Nomos* is translated 'custom' or 'convention,' but was applied to the derivatives of these concepts: law and education.[5]

The ancient Athenians were evidently as perplexed as we are today by the question whether people behaved as they did because of the traits they inherited (i.e. their genetic make-up) or because of the conduct and values they learned.[6] The question pitted the traditional elites against the *dêmos* and the emergent political class that rose up from it. The former generally maintained the beneficial effects of high lineage, the latter tended to view *aretê*, excellence, as a product of *nomos*, or education. The sophists, itinerant teachers with special appeal to the newly rich, touted *nomos* as a matter of course and tended to diminish or disparage the role of inherited characteristics.[7] It was not, however, an either-or question. The elite themselves generally viewed education as a necessary corollary to high birth, or *physis*, in producing a person of noble and honourable character.

Both Odysseus and Philoctetes take Neoptolemus' *physis*, his inherited nature as Achilles' son, for granted and repeatedly invoke it. Their purposes are different, however. Odysseus invokes Neoptolemus' *physis* in order to draw him away from his Achillean heritage so that he can teach him his own ways. Thus, in the midst of his instructions to Neoptolemus to deceive

Philoctetes, he acknowledges that 'by nature you are not the sort of man to utter such words or to contrive evil' (79-80), but urges him to do so in any case. He calls him the son of 'a good man' (96) in practically the same breath as he insists that guile is the only way to obtain Philoctetes' bow. Philoctetes, in contrast, repeatedly appeals to Neoptolemus to act on his Achillean values, not despite them. He argues that Neoptolemus should take him home to Malis because 'to noble men meanness is hateful and generosity brings glory' (475-6). Demanding that Neoptolemus return the stolen bow, he calls on him to 'become yourself' (950).

As the proponent of *nomos*, Odysseus acts as Neoptolemus' tutor and mentor. He makes generalisations in the tone of someone in possession of superior knowledge and wisdom (e.g. 'tongue, not actions, rules all things for mortals', 99; lying is not disgraceful if it 'brings salvation', 109). He urges Neoptolemus to follow his ways (e.g. 'give yourself to me now shamelessly for just a brief portion of the day', 83-4). He issues detailed instructions for how Neoptolemus is to beguile (54-5) Philoctetes and models the technique in his own conduct.

As the proponent of *physis*, Philoctetes does not ask Neoptolemus to follow in his footsteps, does not try to teach him anything, and does not order him around or treat him as a subordinate, but rather places himself in a paternal role. His paternity is emphasised through his repeated address to Neoptolemus as 'my son' or 'my child'.[8] All the characters in the play address Neoptolemus as child or son at one point or other, apparently in a natural response to his youth and immaturity, but Philoctetes' use of the term pervades almost all his conversation with Neoptolemus. With one exception (130), Odysseus addresses Neoptolemus mostly as 'son of Achilles' (4, 50, 1237, 1298).[9] Philoctetes calls him simply 'my son' some forty-eight times, interjecting it into most of their one- and two-line exchanges and several times into most of his longer speeches.[10]

The only time he does not use this appellation is when he is angry at him for refusing to return his bow.[11] This massive interpolation of filial terminology in a play of under fifteen hundred lines conveys the warmth, affection and care of a father, and his expectation that Neoptolemus will return those emotions. In the course of the play, Neoptolemus moves, in somewhat erratic fashion, from being Odysseus' pupil to being Philoctetes' son. The conversion is sporadic and full of reversals, and for much of the play Neoptolemus plays both parts at practically the same time.

The *prologos* traces Neoptolemus' progression from a principled young man to a corrupt one. At the opening of the play, Neoptolemus accepts his junior status vis-à-vis the elder and more experienced Odysseus. He addresses him as 'Lord Odysseus' (26), obediently goes to find Philoctetes' cave, and answers Odysseus' questions with alacrity. Odysseus had informed him that his task was 'to help' (15) him, using a verb (*hyperêtein*) that literally means 'to row', thereby suggesting the relationship between a rower and the commander of a ship. Neoptolemus accepts this.

He protests, however, as soon as Odysseus instructs him to 'steal away' Philoctetes' soul. His ten-line response (86-95) to Odysseus' lengthy 'beguilement' speech (54-85) is his longest in the play thus far and sounds a new note. In an assertion of equality, Neoptolemus addresses Odysseus as 'Son of Laertius' and declares that he was sent as his 'associate', using a word (*xynergatês*) that connotes partnership rather than subordination. Using words built on the root *physis* twice in close succession (88-9), he hammers in his claim that it is not in his nature, as it was not in his father's, to do anything by treacherous plotting. His tone is of naïve pain and surprise that Odysseus would even raise the suggestion.

So what persuades Neoptolemus to relinquish the Achillean heritage he claims? He is not initially moved by Odysseus' warnings that if he does not co-operate he will 'bring grief to all the Argives' and that it will be impossible for him to conquer Troy (67-9), nor by Odysseus' promise of a reputation as 'the most righteous of mankind' as a reward for deceiving Philoctetes (83-5). In his reply, he ignores all three lures: the call to social duty, the opportunity for heroic action, and a hollow reputation for virtue.

The play suggests two answers. One is his immaturity.[12] In the speech under discussion, this is highlighted in particular by his unnuanced declaration that he would rather miss his mark by acting honestly than triumph by cheating. Full of youthful enthusiasm, this is a jejune and unrealistic generalisation with no regard for the complexity of life. Is honest failure really a viable course under any and all circumstances? For example, should a society really forego its interests unless they can be secured above board?

The second answer is self-interest.[13] His fall is triggered by Odysseus' declaration: 'When you do something for profit, it is wrong to hesitate' (111). Neoptolemus picks this up, asking: 'But what profit is it for me if this man should go to Troy?' (112). This question suggests that Neoptolemus is ready to entertain trickery so long as he personally benefits from it. From here on, his self-interest wins out. Now, spurred by the desire for fame that he had earlier rejected, he agrees that it would be worth trying to get Philoctetes' bow if it is essential to capturing Troy (116). Odysseus' assurance that he will win a reputation for being 'clever, and at the same time noble' (119) leads him to declare, in line 120, 'I will do it, putting aside all shame!'

The progression from noble-minded naïf to corrupt young man is very rapid, occurring within less than 150 lines. To a large extent, this rapidity is a dramatic artifice, necessary to reach the main action of the play – the theft and return of the bow – without undue delay. But it also shows Odysseus as an effective teacher and Neoptolemus as a susceptible pupil.

6. Neoptolemus

The first *epeisodion* (219-675) shows Neoptolemus in the role of Odysseus' pupil, yet also leaning towards assuming the role of Philoctetes' son. Like a good pupil, Neoptolemus faithfully carries out Odysseus' instructions (54-65) for stealing away Philoctetes' soul. The gist of his directions is to create a false bond with Philoctetes based on their shared love for Achilles and shared hatred for Odysseus. Neoptolemus does this, using the means that Odysseus had told him to employ. He introduces himself to Philoctetes as Achilles' son (240-1), pretends to view Odysseus and the Atreids as 'evil men' (320-1), and to feel towards them the same rage, desire for revenge and suspicion that Philoctetes feels (324-6, 384, 454-5). He tells Philoctetes that he is sailing home to Scyros and will abandon the Greek host at Troy because the Greeks defrauded him of his father's armour − a story the audience would have recognised as a fabrication. According to the myth, Odysseus was awarded Achilles' arms for his valour and the other person who claimed them was not Neoptolemus but Ajax, whose story Sophocles had dramatised in his play by that hero's name.

The incident also shows Neoptolemus as a talented pupil, as expanding on Odysseus' instructions in the story of the stolen arms. He adds a preface (343-59) in which he fashions an elaborate fiction of how Odysseus and his father's tutor had come to fetch him in a ship decked with flowers and lured him with the promise that he would capture the towers of Troy. Then, instead of recounting the appropriation of the arms in the bare form Odysseus had framed, he creates a dramatic scene, in which he vividly describes himself bursting into tears and rising to his feet in anger and puts quoted speech into the mouths of the Atreids, Odysseus, and himself (364-81). These embellishments demonstrate Neoptolemus' ability to flesh out a tall tale to make it convincing, and suggest that his *physis*, or nature, joins with Odysseus' *nomos* in his fall.

Yet the same embellishments also hint both at Neoptolemus'

inclination to act independently of Odysseus and at the pull that Philoctetes will exercise as father figure. Neoptolemus tells Philoctetes that he was motivated to go to Sigeum by the desire to see his father before he was buried; and how, when he arrived there, the army recognised him as Achilles' son. Then, in describing his altercation with Odysseus, he casts Odysseus in the role of an upbraiding and punitive father and himself as a rebellious son who railed against him. Odysseus, he says, rebuked him for not being with Achilles at his death and 'for speaking with over-bold tongue' (380), and presented his own refusal to give him the arms as a punishment for these offences. These embellishments may be taken as fantasies which convey Neoptolemus' longing for a father, a longing that Philoctetes, rather than Odysseus, will fulfil.

In the remainder of the *epeisodion*, Neoptolemus seems to begin to establish a genuine bond with Philoctetes even as he deceives him. His promise to take Philoctetes home to Malis seems to bring his ruse to completion. Yet it may also be something he would really like to do. He makes the promise right after Philoctetes' moving plea for succour (468-506). Philoctetes had put himself in the position of a suppliant, literally or figuratively getting down on his knees in the traditional gesture of supplication (485 cf. 470), and imploring Neoptolemus not to leave the island without him. It is difficult to know how much Neoptolemus was exploiting Philoctetes' trust and vulnerability, and how much he was genuinely moved by his description of his wretchedness and his plea to 'save me, take pity on me' (501). The Chorus seem to believe that Neoptolemus made the promise in good faith (719-25).

When the Trader arrives, Neoptolemus appears to support Odysseus' plans by playing along with the Trader's fabricated story, though he knows it is false. Yet he may also have sensed that Odysseus had sent the Trader because he was concerned about whether Neoptolemus meant to make good on his promise to take Philoctetes home. So, if he really did intend to keep faith with his new friend, it might be that Odysseus, not Philoctetes, was the person he wanted to mislead. On the other hand, the effect of delaying their sailing after the Trader's exit is to keep Philoctetes on the island long enough to gain possession of his bow. But can we be sure that the wind has not changed, as Neoptolemus claims?

Similar ambiguity characterises the scene with the bow. Neoptolemus shows an almost reverent interest in the famous weapon and asks whether he can hold it. Philoctetes, expressing faith in the young man's *aretê* (virtue, kindness, excellence, nobility, 669), consents on condition that he return it, which Neoptolemus does.[14] After giving it back, Neoptolemus declares, 'I am not sorry to have met you and taken you as a friend' (671). How are we to understand this scene? On the one hand, Neoptolemus' request to touch the bow may be understood as a cynical preparation for filching it later, his handover and return a bitterly ironic prelude to his refusal to return it when he holds it a second time, and his declaration of friendship as yet one more deception among others. Alternatively, we may see his interest in the bow as just what one would expect of a young man of his age and martial ambitions; the bow's handover and return as a vivid visual symbol of the developing bond between the two heroes; and Neoptolemus' statement of friendship, which flows so naturally from the exchange, as an expression of genuine feeling.

The ambiguities regarding Neoptolemus' motives and intentions in these incidents bring home the impossibility of knowing where deception ends and truth begins, if there is truth at all. They also reflect Neoptolemus' mixed motives and his inner confusion about where he really stands between Odysseus and Philoctetes: between the call for expediency and the call for pity.

The interweaving of bonding and deceit continues in the

second *epeisodion*, in which Neoptolemus gains possession of the bow in the course of taking care of Philoctetes. Philoctetes gives him the bow for safekeeping as he is about to fall into the deep sleep that overtakes him during his spasm (763-73). Neoptolemus is rather passive in the matter. He does not ask for the bow. He simply accepts it when Philoctetes asks him to guard it, and pledges, as Philoctetes demands, that he will not allow it to fall into the hands of the Atreids (770-4) – a pledge he keeps.

Both before and after the transfer of the bow, Neoptolemus ministers to Philoctetes, responding solicitously to the sufferer's cries of pain. Up until this point, many of Neoptolemus' utterances have been cerebral and pontifical. A ready example is his declaration, noted above, that he would rather miss the mark honestly than attain it dishonestly (94-5). Another is his self-righteous assertion that he will not tolerate bad men having more power than good ones (456-8). Yet another is his declaration after Philoctetes agrees to let him handle the bow: 'Well, I desire it, but my desire is like this: if it is right for me, I would like it; but if it is not, let it go!' (660-1). Even granting the formality of the tragic style, the declaration comes across as sanctimonious. These and many similarly overblown pronouncements all pointed to Neoptolemus' immaturity, conceit, or insincerity.

A new note is sounded as Neoptolemus responds to Philoctetes' cries of pain by unpretentiously asking him what he should do (757), by addressing him feelingly as 'unfortunate man', and by offering to hold him (759-61). These are direct emotional responses to Philoctetes' suffering, free of bombast and self-importance. They are accompanied by Neoptolemus' first physical contact with Philoctetes, as he gives him his hand in pledge that he will not leave him on the island because of his fit (813) and then, when Philoctetes becomes delirious (815), holds him so that he will not hurt himself (817).[15]

6. Neoptolemus

In the third *epeisodion* Neoptolemus tries to bridge the competing demands that are made on him. He warmly rejoices at Philoctetes' awakening from his spasm (882-3), physically supports him despite his noxious odour (889-93), and voices pity for him. But he is also intent on taking him to Troy and refuses to return his bow. By these actions, Neoptolemus straddles the positions of Philoctetes' son and Odysseus' pupil, not fully committed to either.

Behind his attempt at bridging we may see an intense inner division and mental anguish.[16] For the first time in the play, Neoptolemus articulates the confusion that thus far has emerged only indirectly in his conduct. 'I do not know where to turn my pathless words!' (897) he tells Philoctetes. He confesses the self-disgust that he feels as a man who 'has abandoned his own nature and is doing what does not befit him' (902-3). He declares that he is torn between 'hiding what should not be hidden' and 'uttering the most shameful of words' (909) – that is, between withholding the truth from Philoctetes and telling him the truth in violation of his obligations to Odysseus.

His conflicting allegiances interact as he tells Philoctetes of his intention to take him to Troy. With the warmth and sensitivity that mark his filiality, he states that he is pained by his awareness that the journey will cause Philoctetes grief (912-13). In telling him that the voyage will 'save you from this misery' and that they will go together to 'conquer the plain of Troy' (919-20), he seems genuinely to believe that taking Philoctetes to Troy is the right thing to do and in Philoctetes' own interests. Yet, he also sounds an Odyssean note of rationalising and hiding behind authority, when he claims that 'a stern necessity' (921-2) requires Philoctetes' participation in the defeat of Troy and that he cannot return the bow because 'what is just and what is expedient make me obey those in command' (925-6). Even so, Neoptolemus takes yet another step forward as he responds to Philoctetes' angry tirade (927-62) with his

97

first explicit expression of pity: 'Some strange pity for the man has fallen upon me, not now for the first time, but long since' (965-6). In the second *epeisodion*, he had acted his pity. Here he articulates it. This is an important development, on a par with his telling Philoctetes the truth about the destination of the planned voyage. The ancient Greeks regarded the capacity for pity as essential to humanity. Even amidst the brutalities of the Trojan War, Homer had Patroclus rebuke Achilles for being pitiless in refusing to return to battle in the face of the Achaeans' sufferings (*Iliad* 16.33). Later, the fourth-century orators painted pity as a virtue that attested to the manliness and honour of the jurors. The ancient Greeks reserved their pity for the deserving and for friends, withheld it from the guilty and from enemies. Within these constraints, though, to pity was viewed as the morally right response to suffering.[17] Neoptolemus' expression of pity, in action and words, thus serves as an indicator of his increasing maturity and growth towards ethical manhood. It also marks his assumption of a leadership position vis-à-vis the Chorus. In the *parodos* the Chorus had sung their pity for Philoctetes, whereas Neoptolemus had callously explained his suffering away (see Chapter 3). Now Neoptolemus takes the lead. Moreover, while the Chorus' pity had soon proved superficial, with their participation in Philoctetes' deceit, Neoptolemus' pity is supported by a concrete action: his noncompliance with Odysseus' order to turn over Philoctetes' bow (974-5).[18] His newly articulated pity thus overrides 'what is just and expedient' as his guiding value.

In the *exodos* (1218-471) Neoptolemus completes the transition from Odysseus' pupil to Philoctetes' son, but does not establish an independent identity. This transition occurs in both word and deed. It begins with Neoptolemus hurrying onto the stage, Odysseus at his heels; announcing his intention 'to undo' his former 'error' (1224; cf. 1249-50); and verbally repudiating the Odyssean values and behaviours he had previously accepted. Defining his error as 'obeying you and the entire army' (1226), he rejects the value of obedience to unjust commands. Declaring that it was improper for him to have overcome Philoctetes 'with shameful trickery and guile' (1228), he rejects the use of deceit (120). Announcing that he will return the bow because 'I have gotten it shamefully and not justly' (1234), he sunders the sophistic yoking of virtue and shame and reassumes the sense of shame and moral responsibility he cast off. Proclaiming that being 'just ... is better than being clever' (1246), he rejects Odysseus' sophistic notion of cleverness (118). Refusing to be cowed by Odysseus' threats of violence (1250, 1255, 1257-8), he demonstrates true valour in place of the hollow reputation for valour that Odysseus had promised him if he cheated Philoctetes (118).

His verbal repudiation is completed by action: the highly dramatised return of the bow. The return is delayed by some thirty lines from the time that Neoptolemus announces his intention. The handover is staged in a ritualistic manner, as Neoptolemus tells Philoctetes to 'stretch out your right hand and be master of your bow' (1291-2). And Neoptolemus hands Philoctetes the bow just after or just as Odysseus forbids it (1293-4).

This sequence of events creates a dramatic build-up to the handover, which amplifies its emotional effect and emphasises its multiple significances. It highlights the coming together of words and action in Neoptolemus' behaviour and dramatises his progress from passive noncompliance with Odysseus' earlier order to give him the bow (974-5) to more active defiance. It also casts the handover as a completion of the ritual of giving and returning the bow that had been truncated after Philoctetes gave Neoptolemus the bow for safekeeping. The ritualisation enhances the meaning of the handover as an act that returns to Philoctetes the power and control of which he had been robbed and completes Neoptolemus' bonding with him.

Finally, the dramatisation makes the return of the bow a clear point of division. After the handover, Neoptolemus' sincerity is no longer in doubt, while Philoctetes' refusal to sail to Troy becomes less conscionable.

After repudiating Odysseus' values and ways, Neoptolemus also asserts an independent moral position against some of Philoctetes' values and ways. He does this first by forcibly preventing Philoctetes from shooting Odysseus with his arrow (1300-2). Explaining that shooting his 'hated enemy' (1302-3), as Philoctetes termed it, 'would be honourable neither for me nor for you' (1304), Neoptolemus conveys his disapproval of the unabated hatred, passion and desire for revenge that govern Philoctetes' behaviour.

He also asserts an independent position in his lengthy address aimed at persuading Philoctetes to join the expedition to Troy (1314-47). In some respects, this speech recalls previous utterances. It opens with a critique of Philoctetes' conduct which echoes the Chorus' earlier admonitions. Much like the Chorus, Neoptolemus charges that Philoctetes has brought his suffering on himself, rejects well-meant advice, and treats those who offer it like enemies. Like the Chorus, too, he preaches that persons 'must bear the fortunes given them by the gods' and implies that Philoctetes does not. Moreover, his attribution of Philoctetes' snakebite to divine power in lines 1326-9 recalls his callous explanation for Philoctetes' suffering in the *parodos* (191-200).

In contrast to previous utterances, however, the speech is a passionate personal appeal, very different in tone from Neoptolemus' earlier statements. Neoptolemus presents the request as something he personally would like Philoctetes to do and as a wonderful opportunity for healing and fame through fighting together with himself for a just cause: 'taking Troy, the cause of so much mourning' (1346-7). His accusation that it is not right to 'pardon or pity' persons who are 'wrapped in self-inflicted harm' expresses not only an abstract criticism but also his frustration with Philoctetes' rigidity and the emotional strain of pitying someone who refuses to help himself. His forceful charge that 'you have become savage' borders on rudeness, and is refreshingly free of the self-righteous posturing that marked some of his earlier utterances. His explanation that Philoctetes' wound will never be healed until he comes to Troy of his own accord is informed by sympathy for Philoctetes' 'grievous sickness' and infused by a tone of urgency and conviction, attained with the aid of the vivid image of the rising and setting sun to convey the abstract idea of 'never'. His reiteration of Helenus' prophecy in lines 1337-42 not only provides information but shows him eager to bring evidence that Philoctetes' wound will, in fact, be healed at Troy and that Philoctetes, together with himself, will conquer the city.[19] Furthermore, the speech is punctuated by injunctions urging Philoctetes to heed his words (1325, 1329) and to co-operate willingly now that he knows what he does (1343) – exhortations that convey Neoptolemus' fervent, though futile, hope that if Philoctetes only knew how things really stood, he would join the expedition.

In its function as an effort at persuasion, the speech is the moral means of bringing Philoctetes to Troy that Neoptolemus had initially proposed instead of guile (102). Though the effort fails, it represents both a moral use of eloquence and the apex of Neoptolemus' expression of autonomy and authenticity. It is uninfluenced by Odysseus, free of his double-talk. Its voice is Neoptolemus' own, not the falsetto of a pietistic young man. Towards Philoctetes, the speech is caring and responsible, and its pragmatic and sensible advice conveys the attitude of a mature son who takes care of his father in a role reversal of which the ancient Greeks would have approved as right and proper.[20]

Neoptolemus soon loses his hard-won autonomy, however, as he acquiesces to Philoctetes' insistence that he honour his promise to take him home (1373-408). His capitulation occurs rapidly, as he proves unable to rebut successfully Philoctetes' torrent of objections, not because he lacks answers, but because, as he declares in exasperation, Philoctetes does 'not understand' (1389). In the wake of this recognition, Neoptolemus reverts to his former uncertainty, asking: 'What am I to do if I cannot persuade you of anything I say?' (1393-4). This ingrained uncertainty proves his undoing. In a characteristic flip-flop, he first determines to stop talking and leave the island (1395-6) and then, when Philoctetes continues to insist, accedes with the famous statement, 'If you wish, let us be going!' (1402).

Two related questions are raised by Neoptolemus' acquiescence. One is whether the play presents this as the correct thing to do. On the plus side, the decision represents his choice of friendship over fame and his relinquishing of the self-interest that had precipitated his corruption. On the other hand, his new agreement violates his commitment to Odysseus and the Atreids and places his own countrymen in danger. It represents the fulfilment of his earlier childish and absolutist declaration that he would rather miss his mark by acting honestly than triumph by treachery (94-5). Moreover, it is accompanied by great agitation and worry, as manifested in the rapid, almost breathless staccato of the dialogue of mostly half lines that precedes Heracles' entrance. We may wonder whether only Neoptolemus was uncomfortable with the decision, or Sophocles' audience as well.

The other question is whether Neoptolemus' decision shows the triumph of nature over nurture.[21] A fair number of scholars, who are sceptical of Neoptolemus' transformation, would probably argue that it does not. These scholars cast doubt on the sincerity of Neoptolemus' pity for Philoctetes and of his promise to take him home at the end.[22] Among other things they might point to Neoptolemus' previous inconsistencies, including his theft of the bow soon after he promised to take Philoctetes to

Malis and his refusal to return the bow despite his expression of compassion for Philoctetes (1074-5).

The account of Neoptolemus' development in this chapter is consistent with the view of scholars who believe that Neoptolemus does act honourably in the end and does show a change of heart.[23] This does not, however, mean that the play demonstrates the triumph of *physis* over *nomos*.

Within the play, the supremacy of *physis* is implicit in Philoctetes' interpretation of events. Philoctetes consistently attributes Neoptolemus' good deeds to his *physis*, his bad deeds to Odysseus' teachings. When Neoptolemus returns his bow, he declares, 'you have proven the lineage from which you sprang' (1310-11), but when he stole the bow, he asserted, 'You are not evil, but have apparently come here after learning shameful things from men who are evil' (971-2). In his long rant, he tells Odysseus that Neoptolemus is 'too good' for him, 'knew nothing but that he should obey orders', and was an 'inept and unwilling pupil' (1007-15).

Yet it is not at all clear that Neoptolemus was ever quite as noble-minded as Philoctetes makes him out to be. His rapid corruption, the skill with which he lied, and the talent with which he embellished and dramatised the bare story that Odysseus had told him to relate suggest Neoptolemus' affinity for Odysseus' deceptiveness and point to a combination of Odysseus' teaching and natural inclinations, or *physis*, in his conduct.

Nor does the play quite bear out the notion that *physis* is entirely inherited. Homer's Achilles was incorruptible. Forgoing fame in favour of his personal honour, he turned down Agamemnon's generous gift offer to compensate him for his affront (*Iliad* 9.308-429) and returned to the battlefield after his friend Patroclos was killed. Neoptolemus is corruptible, enticed by the lure of fame. These differences imply reservations about the notion that noble lineage guarantees a noble *physis*. Instead, by showing Neoptolemus as a nobly born youth who succumbs to the demoralisation and corruption of his environment, it may even undercut the entire idea that noble lineage predisposes an individual to noble conduct.

Nor does the play entirely bear out Philoctetes' view that Neoptolemus reveals his inherited nature in returning the bow. The play never quite shows that he chose Philoctetes', and Achilles', principles over Odysseus' sophistry because of his inherited nature. Rather, it shows him increasingly aligning with Philoctetes for affective reasons: in consequence of the warmth and trust that Philoctetes showers him with and the vivid picture of his suffering that he draws. It shows him succumbing to Philoctetes' arguments to take him home because he cannot stick to any other decision in the face of Philoctetes' insistent importuning.

In short, while the play clearly demonstrates the potentially pernicious effects of immoral teachings, what it has to say about *physis* is more ambiguous.[24] This is perhaps appropriate, since the play is not fundamentally about philosophical notions, but the dramatisation of a young man struggling with a moral dilemma and making his choices not in a cognitive fashion, but in accord with his emotional needs for family affiliation.

Sophocles draws Neoptolemus as an adolescent who strives for autonomy, achieves it at points, but does not quite secure it. When he is with Odysseus, he is concerned about the wrong he has done to Philoctetes (1224). When he is with Philoctetes, he is concerned about the opinion of the Greeks if he breaks his pledge to Odysseus (1404). And he repeatedly changes his mind. Neoptolemus' wavering, trying out roles, and rapid changes in emotion are part and parcel of the process of maturation and of discovering who one is.[25] In the course of the play, Neoptolemus gains in maturity, as manifested in the capacity for pity he develops in his acquisition of an authentic voice in place of his earlier bombast and pontification; in the sensible advice that he gives Philoctetes; and in his newly acquired understanding of the real life implications of acting purely on honourable principles. The latter is evident in his concern that the Achaeans will avenge his desertion by attacking his homeland and in his agreeing to set off only after Philoctetes promises to protect it with Heracles' arrows (1406-8). Yet he still lacks the consistency and self-assurance of a mature man. He sees nothing wrong with his frequent changes of mind, and even counters Philoctetes' understandable suspicion when he comes to return the bow with the question, 'Is it not possible to change my mind once again?' (1270). As with others of his age, Neoptolemus' need for guidance and authority remains even as he asserts his independence. It can be argued that this is what makes him susceptible to Philoctetes' persuasions. Although he rejects Odysseus' ways, he is not yet able to steer his own independent course.

7

Heracles

Heracles' entrance in line 1409 brings the action to a different plane and casts a different light on the issues the play treats. Although his entrance is well prepared for and follows logically from what came before, the fact that Heracles is a *deus ex machina* creates a radical disjunction from what preceded it. This has stymied some modern readers, who view the god's intervention as an arbitrary, artificial way of returning the plot to the lines of the known myth, in which Philoctetes participated in the conquest of Troy, and Philoctetes' rapid change of heart as unconvincingly abrupt. Some critics go so far as to dismiss lines 1409-68 as a 'second' ending, inconsistent with the 'real' one that preceded it.[1] Yet, given the frequent use of the *deus ex machina* in Classical tragedy, we may wonder whether the ancient Athenians found it as unnatural as we do.[2] We may also credit Sophocles with having been a skilled enough playwright to have devised a different way of getting Philoctetes to Troy had he wanted to. In fact, it may be argued that Heracles' appearance serves ideological, psychological and religious functions and is essential to the meaning of the play.

Ideologically, Heracles' directives replace the Achillean concept of honour, in which the refusal to forgive a personal insult is a core element, with a concept more appropriate to the needs of the Athenian *polis*.[3] In commanding Philoctetes to go to Troy, Heracles essentially says that he must relinquish his sense of personal injury, however deep or justified, and act towards the common goal. His words to Neoptolemus further emphasise the need for co-operative action: '... you are not strong enough to take Troy without this man, nor is he without you. But like two lions who share the same area, you guard each other' (1434-7). The image pairs the hand-to-hand combat at which Neoptolemus will excel with the less highly regarded archery at which Philoctetes is master. Neither is adequate on its own; both are needed to defeat Troy. The concept of honour that emerges from Heracles' speech is a publicly oriented honour, in which the individual's personal feelings must be subordinated to the common welfare, and moral rectitude cannot be divorced from practical considerations.

This shift parallels changes from Homeric to Athenian society. The great warriors of the Homeric epics were loosely bound in voluntary alliances. Loyalty to the group was important, but not more important than personal glory and spoils. The fifth-century Athenian soldier was a citizen, for whom military service was one of many civic obligations. Moreover, while the best of the Homeric warriors fought in single combat, the fifth-century hoplite fought in a closed phalanx, with shields joined together, spears overlapping, and the success of the engagement dependent on the ability of the phalanx to hold together.[4] Under these circumstances, co-operative endeavour became more important than individual prowess.[5] In both civilian and military life, then, the focus had shifted from the individual to the collective.

Sophocles' long and active involvement in Athens' civic affairs (see Chapter 4), with its inevitable compromises, gives us reason to believe that he would have supported the pragmatism of Heracles' morality. It suggests the primacy he gave to the public interest and also that he would not have supported a young man's opting out of his mandatory military service for the sake of friendship or honesty, as, in a sense, Neoptolemus is ready to do.

Psychologically, Heracles' appearance has a healing function.[6] The play has shown how emotionally difficult it is for a principled individual to rise above the sense of personal injury and to relinquish his hatred and desire for revenge. Heracles enables Philoctetes finally to do so.[7] How? As has been frequently noted, there is nothing new in the inducements of healing and glory that he offers. Nor does his being a god in and of itself confirm the veracity of the prophecy, which Philoctetes had disbelieved. The answer is suggested by Philoctetes' statement: 'O you who have sent a voice I have longed for, you have appeared after a long absence; I will not disobey your words' (1445-7).

Heracles makes his appearance against Philoctetes' great longing both for a father and for a caring god. We hear Philoctetes' longing for his father in his plea that Neoptolemus take him home 'to my beloved father' (492), in his description of his failed efforts to get his father to rescue him (494-9), and in the repeated allusion to the child's word for father (*pappa*) in the pained cries he emits in the agony of his spasm (*papai*: 745-6); *apappapapai*: 754; and *pappapappapai*: 785-6, 792-3). We hear him introducing himself by the double descriptor of 'master of the bow of Heracles, son of Poeas' (262-3), instead of by his patronymic alone, as was the norm. With this introduction, he seems to identify himself as Heracles' son as well as Poeas'.[8] We hear his sense of having been ill treated by the gods and, by implication, his desire for a caring godhead, in his anguished description of himself as 'hateful to the gods' (254), in his feeling that the gods protect evil persons while turning away from righteous men like himself (446-52), and in his complaint that they 'grant me no pleasure' (1020). Heracles' appearance restores Philoctetes' feeling that the gods care for him and satisfies his longing for his father.

Heracles appears as both a father and a god, with a personal, caring interest in the wounded hero. The paternal relationship between Heracles and Philoctetes is implied in the myth of

Heracles' ascension to godhead. According to this myth, Heracles gave Philoctetes (or Poeas) the bow as a reward for lighting his funeral pyre in place of his own son, Hyllus, who refused to do it when he asked him to. In other words, Philoctetes received the bow for acting like a good son to Heracles.[9] Within the play, Heracles acts with special warmth and care towards Philoctetes. He pointedly addresses him before Neoptolemus; he declares that he has left his home in heaven 'especially for your sake' (1413); and he assures him that he will be united with his father Poeas, promising that Philoctetes will take the spoils of the war to him (1428-30).

In addition, Heracles' appearance gives meaning to Philoctetes' suffering. In the play, as in most of the versions of the myth, the snakebite that led to Philoctetes' ten years of agony was precipitated by a minor and inadvert transgression.[10] As the Chorus state, his suffering was undeserved (680-5). Heracles gives it meaning by drawing an analogy between his own trials and destiny and Philoctetes'. Just as he underwent twelve labours 'to win eternal glory', so too Philoctetes' life will be glorious after his sufferings.By giving meaning to Philoctetes suffering, Heracles reconciles Philoctetes to his destiny and enables him to accept it.

Before pointing out the religious functions of Heracles' appearance, I would like to present a minority view (to which I subscribe): that Heracles is Odysseus in disguise. Its proponents argue that, otherwise, *Philoctetes* would be the only one of Sophocles' extant plays to resolve a dilemma in the plot by means of a *deus ex machina* and the only instance in extant Greek literature in which Odysseus fails in an intrigue he engineered.[11]

The view that Heracles is Odysseus would be consistent with Odysseus' conduct throughout the play, where he is a constant, lurking presence, watching Neoptolemus as he engages with Philoctetes.[12] At every point where Neoptolemus favours, or seems to favour, the crippled hero, Odysseus does something to keep him in line. The Trader, or Odysseus disguised as the Trader, and his companion appear right after Neoptolemus agrees to take Philoctetes back home to Malis. Odysseus rushes in himself (974-5) soon after Neoptolemus expresses pity for Philoctetes and gives voice to his moral dilemma; and he turns up again, chasing Neoptolemus onto the stage (1222-3), when the latter is about to return the bow.

The timing of these appearances is such that one can well imagine Odysseus hiding behind a rock, watching and listening to everything Neoptolemus does and says, and coming forward whenever he feels impelled to avert an undesirable turn of events. It would not be the only case of eavesdropping in classical Greek drama (e.g. Aeschylus' *Libation Bearers*, Euripides' *Electra*). Sophocles, who used the device in his *Electra* and *Ajax*, seems to have been fond of it. In these four plays the eavesdropping is explicitly noted in the dialogue; but in the *Philoctetes* it can be inferred.[13] Against this background, it does not seem improbable that Odysseus would similarly show up, only now masked and clothed as Heracles, to intercept Neoptolemus and Philoctetes as they are about to leave the island for their homes. The audience would see him emerging from his hiding place; Neoptolemus and Philoctetes would be unaware of the ruse, and ready to accept Odysseus' message as the god's. Moreover, ancient audiences were sensitive to the way roles were split between actors. As noted in Chapter 1, it is generally believed that the actor who played Odysseus also played the Trader and Heracles. This is logical because in the scenes involved, Odysseus was the only one of the main protagonists who was not on stage. This doubling up would have linked Odysseus not only to the Trader, but to Heracles as well.[14]

The view that Heracles was Odysseus in disguise is also consistent with the message of practicality in Heracles' speech, with its rejection of the Achillean notion of honour, and with the absence of any reference to either Odysseus' trickery or his role in Philoctetes' sufferings, subjects which Odysseus would obviously want to avoid. This reading, however, effectively gives Odysseus the last word and implies that the play endorses his ethos of deception for the sake of victory.

The traditional reading of Heracles as a god, on the other hand, is consistent with Sophocles' reputation as a reverent poet. In about 420-419 BCE he received the healing god Asclepius into his home while a sanctuary was being built (cf. Plutarch, *Numa* 4). After his death he was given a hero cult himself and named Dexion, 'the Receiver' or 'the Welcomer' (of the god).[15] He was also apparently a priest of the hero Halon.

An ending arranged by a divine Heracles supports neither Odysseus' guile nor Neoptolemus' uncivic idealism. It rather asserts the need for divine intervention to resolve the otherwise insoluble dilemmas that the play poses. Up to Heracles' entrance, Sophocles seems to have taken the action to its logical conclusion, given his protagonists' personalities. It was virtually inevitable that Philoctetes, in his all-consuming rage and sense of betrayal, would refuse to go to Troy and that Neoptolemus, with his vacillations and susceptibility to Philoctetes' importuning, would accede to his demand to take him home. These behaviours are not necessarily the 'right' ones, however. Neoptolemus' decision to keep his promise to Philoctetes may be the principled thing to do, but it is also a violation of his civic obligations. Philoctetes' steadfastness may be noble, but it also makes it impossible for him to live in society. Divine intervention not only returns the plot to its traditional course, but also establishes the proper moral hierarchy when values collide. If the play has a message, it is that human beings need the divine to know and to do what is right and to accept the fate that has been given to them.[16]

8

Philoctetes in Our Time

The Philoctetes myth attracted the interest of both Greek and Roman poets throughout antiquity. Sophocles wrote a now lost sequel, *Philoctetes at Troy*, and there are various dramatic and epic treatments that we know of only through allusions or fragments. In the Christian Middle Ages, the story, along with most of the rest of the ancient literary repertoire, was largely ignored. In the Renaissance, when ancient Greek drama was not included in the resurgence of classical learning, its neglect continued.

The revival of the myth began in earnest only in the eighteenth century. It was ushered in by the 1699 publication of François de Salignac de la Mothe-Fénelon's prose fiction, *Suite du quatrième livre de l'Odyssée: ou, Les aventures de Télémaque* (*Sequel to the fourth book of the Odyssey: or the Adventures of Telemachus*), in which Philoctetes tells his story to Odysseus' son Telemachus. In the spirit of French neo-classicism, all the characters are ennobled. Odysseus returns the bow to Philoctetes of his own accord, Neoptolemus is cleared of anything that smacks of sedition, and Philoctetes is thoroughly reconciled to his erstwhile enemy.

Fénelon's work was followed by a rush of translations of Sophocles' *Philoctetes*, into English, French, German, Dutch, Italian and Spanish, and, later, by two adaptations for the stage. The first, by Vivien de Chateaubrun, in 1755, provided Philoctetes with a virgin daughter, with whom Neoptolemus falls in love. It saw seven performances. The second, by

112

LaHarpe, published in 1781, excised the Trader episode, the choral parts, and, like Fénelon, the transfer of the bow. It was performed sixty-eight times by the Comédie-Française between 1783 and 1826.

Along somewhat different lines, Philoctetes figures prominently in *Laocoon* (1866) by the German playwright and critic Gotthold Ephraim Lessing. In this discussion of art and literature, Lessing introduces Sophocles' *Philoctetes* to make the point that the tragic hero can cry and shriek and otherwise express his suffering without losing anything of his stature.

Finally, between around 1770 and 1874, there was a spate of iconographic renditions of Philoctetes. Virtually all of them depict Philoctetes as a great and suffering hero, magnificent in his loneliness and isolation, and remarkably virile and strong looking considering his circumstances.[1] Although interest in Philoctetes seems to have waned in the second half of the nineteenth century, by its end Philoctetes was a fairly familiar heroic figure in educated circles.

The twentieth century saw a further surge of interest in Classical drama. The plays of all three tragedians were translated and produced, in Europe, the United States and Japan, and intensive scholarship and criticism were undertaken.[2] Sophocles' *Philoctetes* was revived as well, through both translations and adaptations.[3] The remainder of this chapter discusses six modern adaptations: five plays and one verse epic. Since an analysis of the works is beyond the scope of this book, the focus will be on the use to which the writers put the myth.[4]

On the verge of the twentieth century, André Gide wrote *Philoctetes: or The Treatise on Three Ethics* (1898). One of Gide's early works, it was probably inspired by Pierre Quillard's (1864-1912) dramatic production of Sophocles' play in Paris in 1896. Gide's work was performed three times, two of them as a reading.[5]

It is a cerebral rendition, which transforms the plot and

113

characters of Sophocles' play in order to contemplate three different ethics. The Chorus and Heracles, not needed for the intellectual schema, are eliminated. Ulysses espouses the ethic of patriotism, in which the good of Greece supersedes all other values and the community is more important than the individual. He marooned Philoctetes on the island, he tells Neoptolemus, because his cries of pain undermined the troops' morale.

Neoptolemus represents the ethic of love. Initially he shares Ulysses' patriotism, to the extent that he is prepared to serve as a sacrifice to the gods in exchange for a Greek victory in Troy; but, like his Sophoclean predecessor, he balks at lying and switches his allegiance to Philoctetes after he gets to know him. In contrast to his Sophoclean namesake, however, self-interest plays no part in his agreeing to deceive Philoctetes; and the driving motive of his transformation is not pity, but love. His love for Philoctetes combines eroticism with a futile quest for virtue, which he hopes Philoctetes will reveal to him.

Philoctetes represents the highest ethic of all for Gide: being true to oneself. Of the three characters, he is the furthest removed from his Sophoclean roots. Free of rancour, he welcomes both Neoptolemus and Odysseus cheerfully. More strikingly, Gide transforms the Sophoclean character who suffers bitterly from his isolation into a figure who glories in it. In his solitude, Philoctetes tells his visitors, he has acquired authenticity, peace of mind and communion with nature that are unattainable in the society of others. Though he is stirred by feelings of love for Neoptolemus, he rejects them when he learns that his visitors were planning to trick him, and refuses to accept Neoptolemus' repentance. When Neoptolemus comes to warn him of Odysseus' scheme to steal his bow after putting him to sleep, he voluntarily swallows the sleeping potion. In his monologue before he falls asleep, Philoctetes rejects devotion to others as the most foolish devotion of all. The play ends with him awakening after his visitors have left, happy that they will never return, and with the island, whose cold and barrenness had mirrored his own disease, bursting into flower and the birds coming down from the sky to feed him.[6] The implication is that the artist can be truly healthy and creative only if he gives up his attachments to others, whether to society as a whole or to loved individuals.

Oscar Mandel's adaptation of the story was first published over half a century later, in 1961, under the title *Island*.[7] It was read on a number of college campuses and over the radio, and twice revised and republished. His version followed shortly upon the first commercial production of the ancient play in the United States in 1959.[8] This was a dual production of Sophocles' text and Gide's, using the same actors. In *The Summoning of Philoctetes*, as the play was called in its last revision, Mandel seems to confront both Sophocles' and Gide's versions. He also borrows from other versions of the myth. From Euripides he takes the idea of a Trojan delegation coming to persuade Philoctetes to join the war on their side; and like Hyginus, he gives Philoctetes a companion.

The central theme of *The Summoning of Philoctetes* is the clash between the many goods of society and the moral purity of living in the wilderness. While Gide's Philoctetes opts for the solitary life, Mandel's chooses society, albeit reluctantly; for society, as Heracles declares at the play's opening, is defined by war. Wherever men come together, they fight.

Odysseus embodies the ambiguities of the social man. He is depicted as an enlightened, modern, democratically elected leader, adored by the Chorus of soldiers, who recount the many benefits of civilisation that he has brought them, his kind treatment of them, and his model behaviour as a husband and father. At the same time, his hands are steeped in blood and destruction. He freely declares his readiness to kill Philoctetes to keep his bow from falling into Trojan hands. To prevail upon

Philoctetes to agree to go to Troy, he kills his companion, Medon, and destroys the home that Philoctetes had built for himself and everything in and around it. He even has two of his own sailors killed, pretending that they are Trojan emissaries slaughtered by his soldiers, so that Philoctetes will believe he has no alternative. This readiness to shed the blood of his own people sharply distinguishes the modern Odysseus from his ancient prototype, whether in Sophocles' depiction or any other.

Mandel's Philoctetes is a sociable and intelligent man, who, along with his companion, has created a cosy, pastoral life for himself. His magic bow, which the play refers to as existing in his mind as well as in the world, is the symbol of his intelligence and technological savvy. These are what the Greeks actually want from him, and what modern societies want from their elites. Like Sophocles' Philoctetes, and unlike Gide's, Mandel's hero longs for human companionship. Thus Medon's murder and Odysseus' destruction of his comfortable home break his spirit, as symbolised by his willfully breaking his bow; and the threat of living companionless on Lemnos induces him to beg Odysseus to take him back. Heracles returns to the stage to commend the decision, though what he envisions for the future is the coming together of the serpent and the eagle, cunning and nobility, rather than of the two lions in Sophocles' text.

The last words in the play are sounded by the poet Demodocus – Mandel's invention – whom his Odysseus had brought along as an assistant in place of Neoptolemus. Odysseus, the political leader, had meant Demodocus to serve him as the state's propagandist, as his name (leader of the people) suggests, and to lure Philoctetes with the temptations of glory and prizes, camaraderie and the warmth of human society. After witnessing Odysseus' brutalities, however, Demodocus has a change of heart and, like Gide's hero, decides to stay on the island by himself. His freedom from the violence and hypocrisy of human society, however, will not bring him joy, as they do

Gide's Philoctetes, but a barren life, where even speech and poetry cease in the absence of anyone to hear them. This conclusion is Sophoclean: human fulfilment occurs in society, however violent and corrupt.

In 1965, the greatly admired East German dramatist Heiner Müller published a much bleaker version of the play, *Philoktet*. This play was first performed in Munich in 1968, and elsewhere thereafter, though not performed in Müller's native East Germany until 1977.[9] The bleakness of *Philoctet* is sounded in the Prologue, where the actor who will portray Philoctetes dons a clown's mask and warns that the play 'lacks a Message' or any lesson that will help on 'a cloudy day'. The background setting of the play is a war whose aims are never mentioned, yet requires that all join in because the vanquished will be slaughtered. The assumption of the concurrence of society and war is similar to the social assumption in Mandel's adaptation, only bleaker because there is no accompanying vision of human warmth and fraternity.

Odysseus is drawn as the eminently resourceful survivor of the Homeric epics. Although he was himself forced to join the expedition against Troy, he says, now that he is a leading commander, he subordinates all to victory. He had marooned Philoctetes because his wound made him useless as a soldier (much as Gide's Odysseus had marooned him because his cries demoralised the forces), but now needs him to lead his sluggish and unmotivated troops into battle. He is averse neither to force nor to trickery, but is honest in his brutality and is sufficiently committed to the Greeks to offer, when Philoctetes threatens to commit suicide, to let Philoctetes kill him instead.

Müller's Neoptolemus is a naïf who hates Odysseus for having stolen his father's arms (something that Müller, unlike Sophocles, depicts as actually having happened), but agrees to deceive Philoctetes and steal his bow because he understands that a Greek defeat will mean his own death as well. Then, like

117

his Sophoclean namesake, he goes back on his deed, and, hoping both to return to his true self and to persuade Philoctetes to join the fight of his own accord, tells Philoctetes of Odysseus' scheme and returns the bow.

Philoctetes is portrayed as hating Odysseus and the rest of the Greeks with a vituperative passion that exceeds even the rage of his Sophoclean prototype, and as having much less warmth and appeal. The limited sympathy he arouses as a victim is quickly doused by his own behaviour. He revels in his power when Odysseus tells him that countless Greeks will die for every moment he holds out. Then, once he has his bow back, he prepares to kill both Neoptolemus and Odysseus, regretting only that he cannot kill Odysseus more than once.

With the murderous depth of Philoctetes' hatred revealed, Neoptolemus' principles are exposed as hopelessly naïve, and his poor judgment, impulsiveness and high-mindedness as a danger to all concerned. He has put his and Odysseus' lives at risk, is forced to kill Philoctetes in self-defence, and, with that act, endangers the lives of the Greeks fighting at Troy, since they will not have the support of Philoctetes' troops.

In the end, Odysseus contrives to use Philoctetes' corpse to rouse his men to fight. He will tell them that Philoctetes was killed by some Trojans after having heroically refused to go over to their side. In a world where there can be no refuge, however barren, it is thus Odysseus who saves the day, with his firm grasp of reality and his endless adaptability and resourcefulness.

Philoctet is one of several plays that Müller wrote on the basis of Greek material. Of all his plays, it is one of the most frequently staged. It is also relatively popular in comparison to the other dramatic renditions of the myth. Its popularity probably stems from the fact that Müller develops his dramatis personae beyond the positions they represent, so that the tensions in his play are within and between characters, not only among ideas. One feels Neoptolemus' barely controlled hatred for Odysseus at the beginning of the play, Odysseus' passionate identification with the war effort, and the resulting tension in their confrontation. At the end, Neoptolemus' shame is conveyed as he realises the stupidity of his actions; and his helplessness and humiliation come across as, obeying Odysseus' directives, he carries Philoctetes' corpse to the ship on his back. Philoctetes' all-consuming hatred is equally palpable.

Thus, even though Müller, like Gide, dispenses with Heracles and the Chorus and pares his play down to three characters with clearly distinct motives and positions, he avoids the schematism that makes Gide's rendition more a treatise than a drama. He makes none of his characters a figure of identification or even likeable; yet by making us feel their emotions, he brings us to recognise their humanity. His play's grim vision of life reflects the bitter twentieth-century experience of East Germany, where the totalitarian oppression of the Communist regime followed upon the totalitarian oppression of the Nazis; yet he brings those of us who live in relatively free and open societies to accept, for the duration of the play, his grim vision of the world.

The Cure at Troy, A Version of Sophocles' 'Philoctetes' is a play written by the Nobel Prize winning Irish poet Seamus Heaney. First produced in 1990 by the Field Day theatre company, Heaney's play follows the text of Sophocles' *Philoctetes* more closely than any of the adaptations discussed above. It also differs from them in its main concern. Whereas they were concerned with alternative approaches to the imperfection of reality, Heaney's play focuses on the self-perpetuation of suffering.

Philoctetes is depicted as a suffering figure whose pain is emblematic of that of human beings in general and of Northern Ireland in particular. Heaney's purpose, however, is less to garner sympathy for Philoctetes than to show how his suffering

– all suffering – is perpetuated by the self-pity and tenacious rancour it spawns. These emotions lead those who suffer, whether individuals or nations, to identify with their pain and thus thwart the possibility of healing and reconciliation.

The conflict between Neoptolemus and Odysseus is subdued in the play, and the Chorus has an enlarged role. It consists of three nebulously drawn female figures who, as in Sophocles' play, identify with Neoptolemus in his mission, but whom Heaney variously terms the 'anima' (e.g. soul, feminine principle) and the voice of Philoctetes' unconscious.[10] They are thus an authoritative voice. They open the play by describing both Philoctetes and Odysseus as persons who, convinced of their rightness, endlessly repeat their mistakes, and they later declare that suffering, inflicted and endured, is the lot of humanity. In this reality, Neoptolemus, with his wavering and changing purpose, comes across not only as scrupulous, but as admirably flexible and better equipped than either Philoctetes or Odysseus to deal with life's vicissitudes.

Redemption is possible in Heaney's play, as in Sophocles'.[11] The Chorus state that, though rare, redemption can be brought about by a miracle. Rather than introducing a *deus ex machina*, however, Heaney transposed Heracles' speech to the Chorus.[12] The source of redemption – of the miracle – in Heaney's play thus becomes our unconscious longing for healing and reconciliation. It is this longing, *The Cure at Troy* implies, that can end the cycle of suffering, whether on the individual level or the political one. At the same time, the redemption is partial and imperfect. Poetry, the agent of the imagination on which redemption depends, has only limited power, the Chorus warn: 'No poem or play or song/ Can fully right a wrong / Inflicted or endured.' This acceptance of partial achievements is also in line with the spirit of Sophocles' *Philoctetes*, where Heracles' reminder to Philoctetes and Neoptolemus to respect the gods in

Troy (1440-4) alludes to the well known acts of brutality and sacrilege that Neoptolemus will soon carry out there.

The Cure at Troy is Heaney's first and, at the time of this writing, still his only dramatic work. Its immediate impetus seems to have been Heaney's participation in the Field Day theatre company, whose *raison d'être* was to contribute, through art and culture, to the resolution of the long and bloody conflict in Northern Ireland between Protestants and Catholics, Unionists and Nationalists.[13] In a controversial passage, Heaney has the Chorus allude with a fair degree of specificity to what may be understood as British oppression in Northern Ireland, where 'The innocent in goals/ Beat on their bars together./ A hunger-striker's father/ Stands in the graveyard dumb./ The police widow in veils/ Faints in the funeral home.' On the whole, however, the play extends its horizons from the 'wound' in Ireland to the wounds that are caused, sustained and cherished in all political conflicts and, in contrast to more strident voices in Field Day, attributes the wounds less to 'colonialism: than to the tendencies of human nature'. In looking beyond the political to the psychological, Heaney's play also comes closer to Sophocles' *Philoctetes* than the other adaptations.

Philoctetes in Vietnam is a simpler interpretation of the story.[14] Staged in 1994, 1995 and 2003 under the direction of Katherine Mendeloff at the Residential College of the University of Michigan,[15] it belongs to the tradition of campus productions and adaptations.[16]

The adaptation was a collaborative effort of the Philoctetes Project, described as 'an ongoing exploration of the parallels between Sophocles' Greek tragedy about an embittered veteran of the Trojan War and the Vietnam era veterans' struggle with the unhealed wounds of their war experience'.[17] The aim of the adaptation was to make Sophocles' play relevant and accessible to modern audiences, while familiarising the post-Vietnam generation of American students with the war that scarred both those who fought it and those who opposed it. Philoctetes' 'festering wound,' writes Mendeloff, 'is an apt metaphor for the Vietnam experience'.[18] It is not, as in the other modern adaptations discussed here, a metaphor for the suffering that marks the human condition.

Philoctetes in Vietnam is an anti-war play. It follows Neoptolemus' conversion from an obedient soldier who joins in the deception of Philoctetes to a morally responsible individual, who returns the bow and prepares to sail for home. The Chorus is a medical evacuation team, each of whose three or four members has a different attitude towards Philoctetes, but whose talk of their experiences in the VA hospital conveys the horror of war. There is no question but that war is wrong and that lying to advance it is equally so.

Heracles is not a figure of redemption, but Odysseus with a loudspeaker. In the 2003 adaptation, his address is full of topical allusions to the Iraq war. He declares himself the 'commander-in-chief' of the Army and orders Philoctetes and Neoptolemus to go fight for security and democracy and against the Axis of Evil.[19] The curtain falls with Philoctetes and Neoptolemus silent and expressionless, trapped by a system bigger than they are. The audience is left to decide for themselves what will happen next.

Omeros (1990), written by the Nobel Prize winning poet and playwright Derek Walcott, was published in the same year that Heaney's play was first produced, and, like Heaney's deals with the intersection of the personal and political. It is a verse epic that transposes Philoctetes to the Caribbean island of Saint Lucia, where Walcott was born. With a French patois form of the name, Philoctete becomes one of a panoply of characters who include both descendants of slaves and ex-colonialists. Several other black characters also have Homeric names, which highlight the ironies of their lives. The Homeric names point to the characters' dispossession, as they come in place of their long forgotten African names; but they also raise the characters to a heroic plane and suggest their enrichment by the cultural heritage of ancient Greece, which, adding to the ironies, is noted both as the source of modern literature and art and as a slave-holding society.

The poem does not follow Sophocles' plot or characterisation, but refers more broadly to the entire Homeric story. Philocte is a poor fisherman who earns extra money by displaying his wound to tourists and grows a yam garden for personal consumption. He is likable, free of rancour, and loves the island. Neither Neoptolemus nor Odysseus takes part in the action. No one comes to fetch Philoctete to fight. The Trojan War is transformed to a personal quarrel between the characters Achille and Hector over the housemaid Helen, and Philoctete's role is that of self-appointed but failed peacemaker.

Yet Walcott's Philoctete shares one major feature with the Sophoclean hero, which does not figure in the Homeric account. This is his painful and foul-smelling wound.[20] The wound, its meaning, and its cure are the focus of Walcott's treatment of Philoctete. As in Heaney's play, the wound exists on three levels: as a personal injury, a political injury particular to a certain group, and the injury and pain that are the human lot. Caused by a rusted anchor, it represents the enduring pain left by the enslavement and transport of the Africans to the New World.[21] 'The swelling,' Philoctete believes, 'came from the chained ankles/ of his grandfathers' on the slave ships (1.III.iii). Yet the wounds that both black and white characters are said to suffer in the poem come from the loss of love, which crosses race and history, much as Philoctetes' wound in Heaney's play represents the wounds of all divided societies.

The odour of his wound precedes Philoctete and warns of his coming, but does not isolate him. Everything has its odour in this poem: failure, loneliness, innocence and the plant that will cure him. Philoctete is poor and crippled and exploited by candidates for office at election time, but he is noble in his patience and power of endurance.

The cure for Philoctete's wound comes through his reconnection with his roots. Its agent is Ma Kilman, the owner of the No Pain café and a local sorceress. Initially she is only able to alleviate the itching and pain of the wound, using a mixture of Vaseline and alcohol. She is able to effect a cure, however, when she remembers the malodorous African roots that her mother had used, literally follows her nose to find them, and, after imploring her African deities for healing and communicating with her ancestors, bathes Philoctete in them. His cure is described as a rebirth.[22]

The rebirth is effected not by returning to Africa, where the descendants of the slaves no longer belong, but by bringing together diverse parts of oneself. Like the slaves, Africa's flora was also brought to the New World, and rebirth comes through the repossession of one's roots wherever one is. The poem ends with other characters cured of their wounds as well.[23] Of all the works, it is the most optimistic.

*

Philoctetes has been produced and adapted less often than other Greek tragedies in modern times. Of Sophocles' seven extant tragedies, it ranks fifth in the number of productions, following *Ajax* and *Women of Trachis*.[24] This may be because it is short on action, because it does not allow the audience the satisfaction of Philoctetes taking personal revenge,[25] or because, lacking in either romantic or familial tensions, it appeals less to our primal emotions than the more popular Greek tragedies. Notwithstanding, the renditions discussed above illustrate the variety of treatments that the ancient story allowed and its adaptability to a variety of modern concerns. The adaptations

change Sophocles' characterisations and some leave out characters altogether, especially the Trader, Chorus and Heracles.
None relates to the question of nature versus nurture, develops
the father-son theme, endows Philoctetes' bow with the rich
symbolic meanings or emotional resonance that Sophocles'
gives it, or traces Neoptolemus' movement towards manhood.

What, then, interests modern authors? The question does not
allow of a single answer. The six works of literature discussed
in this chapter (which do not cover all the modern treatments)
span five countries in space and over a century in time. Only
one of them (Heaney's *The Cure at Troy*) shows any sense of
obligation to Sophocles' text and spirit and any effort to per-
petuate them. In addition to reflecting the unique sensibility
and concerns of each author, the works discussed here grow out
of, and in some cases refer to, different cultural and political
situations. Some authors seem to have been drawn to the clash
of public versus personal values, of expediency versus honesty
in Sophocles' play, and applied this clash to criticise modern
regimes. Some seem to have responded to the powerful image
of human suffering and cure that is central both to the myth
and to Sophocles' play. And others have chosen to present the
intransigent Philoctetes as an example of the dejected citizen
whom the system crushes and makes apathetic. Yet it is in their
very variety that the modern renditions carry on the ancient
tradition, where writers are free to put the story of Philoctetes,
like the stories of other mythological figures, to their own
purposes. They differ from their ancient counterparts in that
they cannot rely on an audience who knew the myth and
possibly other literary renditions as well. What they lose in
resonance, they gain in freedom to depart from the basic story
far more than their ancient predecessors.

Notes

1. Theatre and Performance

1. For general information on Greek tragedy, see Sommerstein, *Greek Drama and Dramatists*.

2. Csapo and Slater, *Context*, pp. 103-21, 287.

3. For a recent detailed study of the institution of the *chorêgoi* see Wilson, *Athenian Institution of the* Khoregia.

4. Cf. Heath, 'Sophocles' *Philoctetes*: A Problem Play?', esp. pp. 151-5.

5. See Griffin, 'Sophocles and the Democratic City'.

6. See also Csapo and Slater, *Context,* pp. 289-90.

7. Csapo and Slater, *Context*, pp. 286-7, 290-3; Taplin, 'Comedy and the Tragic', pp. 193-4.

8. For the uncertainty of when the subsidy started and the different ticket price, see discussion in Csapo and Slater, *Context,* pp. 287-8, Pickard-Cambridge, *Dramatic Festivals*, pp. 266-8.

9. Csapo and Slater, *Context,* pp. 290, 301-5.

10. Pickard-Cambridge, *Dramatic Festivals*, pp. 68-70.

11. Pickard-Cambridge, *Dramatic Festivals*, pp. 97-8.

12. Wiles, *Tragedy in Athens,* pp. 44-52; for the variety of interpretations of the various remains, see Moretti, 'The Theater of the Sanctuary of Dionysus Eleuthereus in Late Fifth-Century Athens'.

13. Beer, *Sophocles and the Tragedy of Athenian Democracy*, pp. 25-9, argues that by *skênographia* Aristotle meant the verbal setting of the time, space and topography typically found in the prologues of the plays.

14. The Greek terms used here to denote the various parts of the play probably post-date the fifth century. I use them because they are conventional in literature and also because they remind us that Greek tragedy is a distinct genre whose parts are not the same as those of modern Western drama.

15. Beer, *Sophocles*, pp. 4-5, maintains that the Chorus represented the polis 'onstage'. For a well-argued modification of this claim, see

Griffin, 'The Social Function of Attic Tragedy', pp. 42-3. For discussion of whether the Chorus generally embodied a 'civic voice', see Gould, 'Tragedy and Collective Experience'; Goldhill, 'Collectivity and Otherness – The Authority of the Tragic Chorus: Response to Gould', pp. 244-56; Taplin, 'Comedy and the Tragic', pp. 193-4.

16. An obvious exception is Aeschylus' *Eumenides*, where the action moves from Delphi to Athens and could not have been completed in a day.

17. The long-standing supposition that the masks were a relic of the Dionysian rites out of which the tragedies are thought to have developed has been recently challenged by Halliwell, 'The Function and Aesthetics of the Greek Tragic Mask', pp. 197-202. For different views on masks and their function, see Wiles, *Tragedy in Athens*, p. 77, Halliwell, 'The Function and Aesthetics of the Greek Tragic Mask', Marshall, 'Masking Conventions', and Winkler, 'The Face of Tragedy'.

18. Winkler, 'The Face of Tragedy', p. 47.

19. Marshall, 'Masking Conventions', pp. 193-4.

20. Pickard-Cambridge, *Dramatic Festivals*, pp. 180-209.

21. Pollux, *Onomasticon* iv,116. Pickard-Cambridge, *Dramatic Festivals*, pp. 202-3; Csapo and Slater, *Context*, p. 393.

22. For the uncertainty of this claim, however, see Csapo and Slater, *Context*, pp. 221-2, 226-7.

23. Cf. Easterling, 'Actor and Voices', 'Actors as Icon'; Hall, 'Actor's Song in Tragedy' and 'The Singing Actors of Antiquity'; Pavlovskis, 'The Voice of the Actor in Greek Tragedy', p. 113; Damen, 'Actor and Character in Greek Tragedy', p. 318.

24. Scholion to Aristophanes *Clouds*, 1267. Hall, 'The Singing Actors of Antiquity', p. 9.

25. Taplin, 'Mapping', pp. 16-19, 179.

26. For different views of the placement of the entrances, see Robinson, 'Topics', pp. 37-9; Dale, 'Seen and Unseen on the Greek Stage', pp. 127-8, cf. Taplin, 'Mapping', p. 47 n. 16; Wiles, *Tragedy in Athens*, pp. 153-4.

27. See Taplin, *The Stagecraft of Aeschylus*, p. 370.

28. Aeschylus, *Eumenides*, in which there is a movement from Delphi to Athens, is an exception. For the importance of the Chorus' constant presence see Gould, 'Tragedy and Collective Experience', esp. pp. 232-3.

29. E.g. Robinson, 'Topics', pp. 36-8.

30. Dale, 'Seen and Unseen on the Greek Stage', pp. 127-8.

31. Pavlovskis, 'The Voice of the Actor in Greek Tragedy'. For the congruity of the characters portrayed by an actor, see Damen, 'Actor and Character in Greek Tragedy', pp. 321-6.

32. There is textual evidence for both interpretations. See Avery, 'One Ship or Two at Lemnos?', pp. 18-19, and Raubitschek, 'A Note on the *Philoctetes* (1402)', p. 198. It may be noted that the heroes of the Homeric epics are said to travel in their own ships. On the other hand, Dio Chrysostom's description of Sophocles' Chorus as consisting of Odysseus' and Neoptolemus' sailors implies that Dio assumed there was only one ship (52.15).

33. See Easterling, 'Transmission of the Text', pp. 164-73.

2. The Myth

1. For the view that Sophocles was not answering Euripides, see, for example, Webster, *Philoctetes*, p. 5. For the view that Sophocles was answering intentionally his predecessors' versions, especially Euripides', and expected the audience to recognise the differences, see Kittmer, 'Sophoclean Sophistics', pp. 24-6.

2. For the place of myth and poetry in that education, see Beck, *Greek Education: 450-350 BC*, pp. 17-71.

3. The vase paintings provide only the barest, most basic information and add nothing to the literary references. For example, a red-figure vase, 490 BCE, depicts Philoctetes bitten by a snake; a Stamnos from Attica, c. 460 BCE, by Hermonax, shows the Wounding of Philoctetes; a red-figure psykter, c. 460 BCE, depicts Heracles lying on his lion-skin atop his funeral pyre and handing his bow and quiver to Philoctetes. For further discussion, see Robertson, *Art of Vase-Painting*, pp. 196, 198, 204, 238; Ferrari, 'Myth and Genre on Athenian Vases'. For a full catalogue of the depiction of Philoctetes in art see *Lexicon Iconographicum Mythologiae Classicae*, vol. VII.1, pp. 376-85; vol. VII. 2, pp. 321-6.

4. I am indebted to Mandel's thorough survey of the mythic background of the *Philoctetes* (*Philoctetes and the Fall of Troy*, pp. 3-45).

5. See Cameron, *Greek Mythography in the Roman World*, passim.

6. Heracles alludes to these brutalities in lines 1440-4, where he warns Neotpolemus and Philoctetes to remember to show reverence for the gods in Troy. See for example, Winnington-Ingram, *Sophocles*, pp. 302-3; Rehm, *Radical Theatre*, p. 85.

7. For recent discussion of Euripides' *Philoctetes*, see Müller, *Philoktet: Beiträge zur Wiedergewinnung einer Tragödie des Euripides aus der Geschichte ihrer Rezeption; Euripides: Philoktet.*

8. E.g. Mandel, *Philoctetes*, pp. 21-2.

9. Rose, 'Teachings of the Sophists'; Rehm, *The Play of Space*, p. 139. See pp. 138-41 for a comprehensive discussion of Sophocles' decision to have the island unpopulated.

10. Scholia to Lycophron, *Alexandra* 1268; *The Sack of Ilion* 1.

3. The Play

1. The Greek word *ekklepseis*, here rendered 'steal away,' may also be translated as 'beguile,' 'ensnare' and 'deceive'.

2. There is considerable debate in the literature as to the precise content of the prophecy and about what the various characters know about it at different points of time. For different views on Sophocles' treatment of the oracle in *Philoctetes*, see Hinds, 'The Prophecy of Helenus in Sophocles' *Philoctetes*'; Bowra, *Sophoclean Tragedy*, p. 268; Knox, *The Heroic Temper*, pp. 126-7; Linforth, 'Philoctetes: The Play and the Man', p. 103; Robinson, 'Topics', p. 47; Easterling, '*Philoctetes* and Modern Criticism', pp. 26-7; Kittmer, 'Sophoclean Sophistics', pp. 24-9. The view of this book is that Sophocles has characters relate different parts of the prophecy as suits their needs.

3. It has been suggested that all three methods fail. Knox, *Heroic Temper*, pp. 119-20; Garvie, 'Deceit, Violence, and Persuasion in the *Philoctetes*'. The matter may not be so clear, however. Force is never really tried. Trickery works until Neoptolemus decides to tell Philoctetes the truth. And while Neoptolemus cannot persuade Philoctetes, Heracles does.

4. King, *Achilles*, p. 73 suggests that the morality of Sophocles' day would not have seen anything reprehensible in Neoptolemus' suggestion to exploit Philoctetes being a cripple. It is hard to see the grounds for this claim.

5. For the question of whether Neoptolemus had his own ship or sailed with Odysseus, see Chapter 1 n. 32.

6. The possibility that the Trader is Odysseus in disguise was raised by Ahl, *Sophocles' Oedipus*, p. 211 and further developed by Roisman ('Ever-Present Odysseus', pp. 44-9), who argues that, with his cautious and suspicious nature, Odysseus would be loathe to leave to a mere sailor the important mission of making sure that Neoptolemus does not spoil his scheme by taking Philoctetes to Malis.

7. For the problematics of the late announcement that Philoctetes' presence is required for the fall of Troy, see Lesky, *History of Greek Literature*, pp. 291-2; Gill, 'Bow, Oracle, and Epiphany in Sophocles' *Philoctetes*', pp. 137-46, argues convincingly for Neoptolemus' intuitive understanding as the plot evolves of the necessity for Philoctetes' presence.

8. Wilamowitz-Moellendorff, *Die dramatische Technik des Sophokles*, pp. 281-3; Waldock, *Sophocles the Dramatist*, p. 204, and Podlecki, 'The Power of the Word in Sophocles' *Philoctetes*', p. 239, claim that the Trader's intervention adds nothing to the plot. Biggs, 'The Disease Theme in Sophocles' *Ajax, Philoctetes and Trachiniae*', pp. 232-5, contends that it is necessary to bring on Philoctetes' fit. Philoctetes, however, says that he had fits on other occasions as well.

9. See Kittmer, 'Sophoclean Sophistics', pp. 20-1.

10. See Kittmer, Sophoclean Sophistics', p. 22.

11. See Rehm, *The Play of Space*, pp. 152-3, and bibliography. Rehm maintains that Philoctetes sinking to the floor, as he terms Philoctetes' fainting, is 'a rare occurrence in the tragic theater'.

12. Knox, *Heroic Temper*, p. 133 and Hogan, *Commentary*, to 973-7.

13. For the view that Odysseus is bluffing, see Jebb, *Sophocles*, p. xxviii; Hinds, 'The Prophecy of Helenus', pp. 177-9; Hoppin, 'What Happens in Sophocles' 'Philoctetes'?', esp. pp. 24-6. For the view that it was not a bluff, see Knox, *Heroic Temper*, p. 134; Robinson, 'Topics', pp. 44-51; Taplin, 'Mapping', p. 35 n. 24; Calder, 'Sophoclean Apologia: *Philoktetes*', pp. 160-1; Kamerbeek, *The Plays of Sophocles*, on 1054-6; Ussher, *Sophocles, Philoctetes*, on 1054-6. Hogan, *Commentary*, on 1047-61, argues that the point is that Neoptolemus 'acts as if he believes him (1073-80)'.

4. Contexts

1. See, for example, Kirkwood, *Sophoclean Drama* and Bowra, *Sophoclean Tragedy*.

2. The relevant works will be cited in the course of the book, but see, for example, Goldhill, 'Great Dionysia and Civic Ideology'; for a critique of Goldhill's claims, see Griffin, 'Social Function', esp. pp. 46-50.

3. Knox, *Heroic Temper*, p. 52. For Homer as a source of inspiration for Sophocles, see Miller, '*ho philomeros Sophocles* and Eustathius'.

4. Marrou, *A History of Education in Antiquity*, pp. 21-34, 70-1, 89-90, 109, 223-42; Goldhill, *Reading Greek Tragedy*, pp. 138-43.

5. For other Homeric paradigms and echoes in the play, see Fuqua, 'Thematic Structure of Sophocles's *Philoctetes*'; Davidson, 'Homer and Sophocles' *Philoctetes*', p. 122.

6. Beye, 'Sophocles' *Philoctetes* and the Homeric Embassy', pp. 64-5.

7. For the antitheses of word and deed and love and hate as formative matrixes of the play, see Minadeo, '*Theme and Plot in the Philoctetes*'.

8. For Odysseus' skill in deception, see also Hesk, *Ajax*, pp. 36-8.

9. See, for example, the figures of Nestor (e.g. *Iliad* 1.247-84, 4.313-25, 8.80-91), Diomedes (*Iliad* 5.1-351, 9.669-713), and Neoptolemus (*Odyssey* 11.510-37). Cf. Roisman, 'Nestor the Good Counselor'.

10. For Neoptolemus in the *Odyssey*, see Roisman, 'Appropriation', pp. 131-6.

11. See Rehm, *Radical Theatre*, pp. 82-4, for a discussion of how the repetition of the question heightens the play's dramatic tension.

12. E.g. the conflict between Antigone and Creon in his *Antigone*, and the contentious disputes between Oedipus and Teiresias in *Oedi-*

pus the King. For the latter, see Roisman, 'Teiresias, the Seer of *Oedipus the King*'.

13. Goldhill, *Reading Greek Tragedy*, pp. 138-67; Easterling, 'The Tragic Homer'; Shucard, 'Some Developments in Sophocles' Late Plays of Intrigue'.

14. E.g. Goldhill, *Reading Greek Tragedy, passim.*

15. On the *polis*, see Hansen, *Comparative Study of Thirty City-State Cultures*, and Murray and Price, *Greek City: From Homer to Alexander*, especially chs 8-14.

16. For democratic ideology see Ober, *Mass and Elite in Democratic Athens*, esp. pp. 38-40, 54, 82, 86, 94.

17. E.g. Aeschylus' *Seven Against Thebes*, Sophocles' *Antigone, Electra* and *Oedipus at Colonus*, Euripides' *Phoenician Women*.

18. For the terms and their meanings, see esp. Hansen, *The Athenian Ecclesia*, pp. 1-24, 93-127.

19. Kennedy, *Art of Persuasion*, pp. 13-51; Usher, *Greek Oratory*, pp. 296-7; Halliwell, 'Between Public and Private: Tragedy and Athenian Experience of Rhetoric', pp. 121-6.

20. Kennedy, *Art of Persuasion*, pp. 27-9.

21. For a detailed account of the sophists' teachings, see Guthrie, *The Sophists*. Shorter accounts are available in the *Oxford Classical Dictionary*. See also Rose, 'Teachings of the Sophists'.

22. Jameson, 'Politics and the *Philoctetes*'. For the opposite view, see Vickers, 'Alcibiades on Stage: *Philoctetes* and *Cyclops*', pp. 172-87. For general views on the validity of extracting political contextual evidence from tragedy, see Pelling, 'Conclusion'.

23. Jameson, 'Politics and the *Philoctetes*', p. 217; Kennedy, *Art of Persuasion*, p. 279 n. 257 contends that this was not Sophocles the playwright.

5. Odysseus and Philoctetes

1. E.g. Robinson, 'Topics'; Rose, 'Teachings of the Sophists'.

2. See Heath, 'Sophocles' *Philoctetes*: A Problem Play', pp. 142-51.

3. The earliest versions of the oath that have come down to us are from the fourth century, so we cannot know whether the same oath was sworn in the fifth century. However, the idea of obedience constrained by justice was consistent with Athens' view of itself as a democracy.

4. For sophistic influence in Sophocles' portrayal of Odysseus, see Craik, 'Sophocles and the Sophists'; Blundell, 'Moral Character'. Cf. also Knox, *Heroic Temper*, pp. 124-6.

5. See also Blundell, 'Moral Character', p. 314.

6. Taplin, 'Significant Actions', p. 37, points out that 'Odysseus in this scene is on stage less than ten lines, and rushes off in silence. Characters in Greek tragedy do not run off stage under threat of force.'

7. Nussbaum, 'Consequences and Character'.

8. Blundell, 'Moral Character', p. 308, suggests that Odysseus will gain spoils, but the play makes no mention of this.

9. E.g. Rose, 'Teachings of the Sophists', p. 100: 'Philoctetes is clearly the best human being left alive.'

10. This follows his prayer for death during his spasm (797-8) and precedes his wish for death in lines 1158, 1208-9. It should be noted, however, that while there is no doubt about his intention at this point in the play, his earlier prayer for death was made when he was in agonising pain, when people do not always mean what they say.

11. Cf. Garland, *The Greek Way of Death*, pp. 95-9; Hesk, *Ajax*, pp. 97-9.

12. See J. Roisman, *Rhetoric of Manhood*; for honour see ch. 3 and *passim*; for freedom, pp. 133-4.

13. For the problematics of the choral corroboration and various views explaining the Chorus' stance see Bers, *Sophocles*. See also O'Higgins, 'Narrators and Narrative', p. 50 n. 19. For the Chorus' 'strategy of deceit' (p. 21) see Kittmer, 'Sophoclean Sophistics', pp. 21-4.

14. For the role of the Chorus in the play see Gardiner, *The Sophoclean Chorus*, pp. 13-49. For recent discussion of the role of the Chorus in Greek tragedy and the idea of authoritative voice, see Gould, 'Tragedy and Collective Experience', and bibliography, Goldhill's response 'Collectivity and Otherness – The Authority of the Tragic Chorus: Response to Gould', and Taplin, 'Comedy and the Tragic', pp. 193-4.

15. Wilson, 'Philoctetes: The Wound and the Bow', views Philoctetes' wound as symbolic of his rage and inability to relate to society.

16. Good will (*eunous*) is one of the terms used to denote personal loyalty in the Homeric epics; see Roisman, *Loyalty*, pp. 1-84. Aristotle calls it a crucial character trait for a speaker to be persuasive (*Rhetoric* 1378a).

17. On friendship, see Blundell, 'The Moral Character of Odysseus', p. 308 and bibliography; Konstan, *Friendship in the Classical World*, pp. 56-9, 79-82, and *passim*; Rose, 'Teaching of the Sophists', pp. 64-80 for the importance of friendship in the play. For a general study of the subject, see G. Herman, *Ritualised Friendship and the Greek City*.

18. See Chapter 3 n. 13.

19. Knox, *Heroic Temper*, pp. 119-20.

20. Cf. King, *Achilles*, pp. 66-77.

21. King, *Achilles*, pp. 77-80.

6. Neoptolemus

1. Vidal-Naquet regards Neoptolemus' decision to take Philoctetes home as a rejection of the civic values of the polis in favour of the values of the household: Vernant and Vidal-Naquet, *Myth and Tragedy*, p. 173; cf. Vidal-Naquet, *The Black Hunter*, pp. 85-105.

2. Cf. Vidal-Naquet, 'Sophocles' *Philoctetes* and the Ephebeia' and Goldhill, 'The Great Dionysia and Civic Ideology', pp. 118-23. Rehm, *The Play of Space*, pp. 139, 351 n. 116, notes that in 409 BCE the *ephebeia* was not yet in existence.

3. See Roisman, 'Appropriation', for the competition between Odysseus and Philoctetes to appropriate Neoptolemus as a son. In that paper, I presented both Odysseus and Philoctetes as aspiring fathers. Since then, I have come to the conclusion that Odysseus is better seen as a tutor. This does not invalidate the earlier claim; elements of both roles are present. See Knox, *Heroic Temper*, pp. 122-4, and Segal, *Tragedy and Civilization*, p. 299.

4. Whitby, 'Telemachus Transformed?', claims that Sophocles models the development of Neoptolemus on Homer's portrayal of Telemachus.

5. Guthrie, *The Sophists*, ch. x and *passim*. For the range of meanings of *nomos*, see Humphreys, 'Law, Custom and Culture in Herodotos'. For the antithesis between 'nurture' and 'nature' as the 'underlying organisational principle' of the play, see Fuqua, 'The Thematic Structure of Sophocles's *Philoctetes*', pp. 55, 70, 215-16.

6. Pindar, *Olympian* 9.100-4, cf. *Pythian* 8.44-5, for example, holds that only noble lineage is essential to nobility of character.

7. Rose, 'Teachings of the Sophists', pp. 85-7.

8. The Greek words *teknon* and *pais* can translate either.

9. For the nuances in calling Neoptolemus the son of Achilles, see Michelakis, *Achilles in Greek Tragedy*, pp. 162-4.

10. 236, 249, 260, 268, 276, 284, 300, 307, 315, 327, 337, 466, 468, 478, 484, 533, 578, 628, 635, 658, 662, 733, 742, 745 (twice), 747, 750, 753 (twice), 776, 782, 799, 804, 805, 807, 811, 869, 875, 878, 879, 889, 896, 898, 914, 932, 967, 981, 1295, 1301, 1310, 1367, 1399.

11. Then he addresses Neoptolemus by the formal and distancing 'seed of Achilles' (1066) or 'offspring of a most noble father' (1284).

12. Inoque, 'Sight, Sound, and Rhetoric', p. 220, describes Neoptolemus as a naive, inexperienced youth who has not yet been exposed to the ways of men.

13. Cf. Kott, *The Eating of the Gods*, p. 178: 'Neoptolemus is a young man who is devoured by ambition and whose one unchanging trait is instability.'

14. Hogan, *Commentary*, to 671-4 and Winnington-Ingram, *Sopho-*

cles, p. 286 n. 20, contend that Neoptolemus does not actually take the bow at this point.

15. Jebb, *Sophocles*, on 814-18; Webster, *Philoctetes*, on 814-15. For discussion of the progression of physical contact in the play and how it marks the turning points of he developing drama, see Kaimio, *Physical Contact in Greek Tragedy*, pp. 83-5.

16. Ryzman, 'Neoptolemos', maintains that Neoptolemus had to undergo a personal crisis in order to return to his true nature.

17. On the importance of pity, see Konstan, *Pity Transformed*, pp. 52-3, 125-7.

18. Knox, *Heroic Temper*, p. 133, maintains that in line 974 Neoptolemus must be in the very act of handing the bow to Philoctetes.

19. This is the fourth and most detailed repetition of the prophecy in the play (68-9, 191-200, 603-13). Scholars have noted that the play is very unclear about how Neoptolemus obtained his information (e.g. that Philoctetes received the snakebite at Chryse's shrine, that he will be healed only at Troy, and that Troy will be taken in the summer). See also Chapter 3 n. 2. It may be noted that Sophocles similarly provided no explanation for how the Chorus had information about Philoctetes (e.g. that he was a suspicious man) before Neoptolemus told them anything. Such details, which lack thematic significance and are not important to the characterisation of the dramatis personae, apparently did not matter to Sophocles.

20. Hesiod names children's lack of respect for their aged parents among the signs of deterioration in the Iron Age (*Works and Days* 185-7).

21. For Neoptolemus as a developing character who comes only slowly to recognise and act on his innate qualities, see Ryzman, 'Neoptolemus', pp. 35-41.

22. Calder, 'Sophoclean Apologia', pp. 162-7; Raubitschek, 'Note'. The ancient commentator (scholiast) wrote with respect to Neoptolemus' famous 'let us be going' (*steichômen*, 1402): 'To the fatherland; but he is deceiving him and wishes to take him to Troy'. For a summary of the views about the sincerity of Neoptlemus' pity throughout the drama see Easterling, '*Philoctetes* and Modern Criticism'.

23. E.g. Wilson, 'Philoctetes: The Wound and the Bow'; Robinson, 'Topics', pp. 51-3; Vidal-Naquet, 'Sophocles' *Philoctetes* and the Ephebeia', pp. 161-175. Rose, 'Teachings of the Sophists', pp. 77-9.

24. For the view that Neoptolemus does live up to his *physis*, see Blundell, 'The *phusis* of Neoptolemus', p. 145: '*Phusis* is a potential, and a noble *phusis* may manifest itself in various ways .... He lives up to his noble *phusis* ... combining the best of Achillean honesty and Odyssean persuasiveness ....'

25. Cf. Grinder, *Adolescence*, pp. 23-147.

7. Heracles

1. E.g. Robinson, 'Topics', pp. 51-6.

2. Linforth, 'Philoctetes: The Play and the Man', pp. 150-4. Euripides' *Medea, Orestes* and *Electra*, for example, all have a *deus ex machina*.

3. Pucci 'Gods' Intervention and Epiphany in Sophocles', p. 37, argues that Heracles' directive 'forces the tragic action to ... retrieve the life and thought patterns of the epic world and its narrative'.

4. For a more qualified view of the Homeric warfare which assumes in addition a possibility of 'an embryonic hoplite phalanx in the process of development' (691), see Van Wees, 'Homeric Warfare'.

5. Goldhill, *Reading Greek Tragedy,* pp. 144-5.

6. For a detailed discussion of the propriety of Heracles, out of all the gods, being the one to lure the intransigent hero back into society, see Greengard, *Theater in Crisis*, esp. pp. 88-99.

7. See Biggs, 'The Disease Theme in Sophocles' *Ajax, Philoctetes and Trachiniae*', pp. 231-5, for Philoctetes' final re-association with the Greek army as the ultimate cure for his disease, which is poisonous hatred of those who have abandoned him.

8. The play further supports this dual paternity. In the midst of his spasm, he recalls the myth by asking Neoptolemus to burn him as he had burned Heracles after the latter's death (799-805). The Chorus refer to Philoctetes' home as the place where Heracles 'joined the gods as a god' (676-729). Neoptolemus addresses Philoctetes as 'son of an Oetaean father' (453); Mount Oeta was in Poeas' kingdom, and also the place of Heracles' funeral pyre.

9. See Avery, 'Heracles, Philoctetes, Neoptolemus', pp. 290-4.

10. Cf. Sommerstein, *Greek Drama and Dramatists*, p. 47.

11. Errandonea, 'Filoctetes' (1955), pp. 122-164; (1956), pp. 72-107; Lattimore, *Story Patterns in Greek Tragedy*, p. 92 n. 35, cf. pp. 43-5.

12. See Ahl, *Sophocles' Oedipus*, pp. 210-11; Roisman, 'Ever-Present Odysseus'.

13. Taplin, *Tragedy in Action*, pp. 131-3.

14. See Kittmer, 'Sophoclean Sophistics', pp. 25-6; Rehm, *The Play of Space*, pp. 151-2.

15. Lesky, *Greek Tragic Poetry*, p. 118.

16. Parker, 'Through a Glass Darkly', pp. 22-3.

8. Philoctetes in Our Time

1. All of the above is drawn from Mandel, *Philoctetes*, pp. 134-9. This book offers a detailed survey of the treatment of the Philoctetes story in literature and art from ancient times through the time of the book's publication in 1981. Taplin, 'Sophocles' *Philoctetes*, Seamus

Heaney's, and Some Other Recent Half-Rhymes', also provides useful insights about both pre-and post-twentieth-century productions and adaptations of the play. For more information about productions of the play, see the Oxford archive for performance http://www.apgrd.ox.ac.uk/. For a complete account of the Philoctetes legend in art from the fifth century BCE to the third century CE, see Milani (1879 and 1882).

2. Mandel (1981) p. 153. For detailed accounts, see Hartigan, *Greek Tragedy*, and Macintosh, 'Tragedy in Performance'.

3. Mandel, *Philoctetes*, pp. 154-250, notes six adaptations up to 1981, and prints three of them in full: *Philoctetes or The Treatise on Three Ethics* (1898) by André Gide, *The Summoning of Philoctetes: A Tragedy* (1961) by Oscar Mandel; *Philoctetes* (1965) by Heiner Müller. Rush, 'Modern Interpretations of Sophocles' *Philoctetes*', pp. 23-7, notes another seven theatrical productions of various closeness to the original between 1981 and 1986.

4. A more detailed discussion of the treatment and uses of Sophocles' play in three of the modern renditions of the myth discussed in this chapter (Heiner Müller's *Philoktet*, Seamus Heaney's *The Cure at Troy*, and Derek Walcott's *Omeros*) is provided by Taplin, 'Sophocles' *Philoctetes*, Seamus Heaney's, and Some Other Recent Half-Rhymes'.

5. Mandel, *Philoctetes*, p. 148. For a summary of Gide's play, see Rush, 'Modern Interpretations', pp. 14-15.

6. Wilson, Philoctetes: *The Wound and the Bow*, p. 289, maintains that Gide's Philoctetes is at once 'a moralist and an artist, whose genius becomes purer and deeper in ratio to his isolation and outlawry'.

7. Mandel, *Philoctetes*, pp. 181-2.

8. Hartigan, *Greek Tragedy*, p. 135.

9. For the play, translated by Mandel in collaboration with M. Kelsen Feder, see Mandel, *Philoctetes*, pp. 223-50. For its summary and comparison with Sophocles, see Rush, 'Modern Interpretations', pp. 16-17. For the use of Greek tragedy to explore current political and ideological issues in post-WWII Europe, see Macintosh, 'Tragedy in Performance', pp. 318-21. On Müller's *Philoktet* and other plays based on Greek tragedies, see also Flashar, *Inszenierung der Antike*, pp. 241-4.

10. Letter to Tony Taccone, in Heaney's *The Cure at Troy*, p. 172.

11. Deane, 'Field Day's Greeks (and Russians)', pp. 156-8, maintains that Heaney follows Wilson's reading in *The Wound and the Bow*, which does not allow a tragic conclusion. Walton, 'Hit or Myth: the Greeks and Irish Drama', p. 16, claims that Heaney's approach offers 'seeds of hope for reconciliation and even redemption'. Cf. Heaney's comments, *The Cure at Troy*, pp. 176-8.

12. Heaney, *The Cure at Troy*, pp. 172-3.

13. www.english.emory.edu/Bahri/FieldDay.html.

14. In 1994 The Aquila Theatre Touring Company staged Sophocles' *Philoctetes* as translated by Peter Meinecke and directed by Robert Richmond.

15. I wish to thank Katherine Mendeloff for her generosity with her time and good will in talking to me and sending me material.

16. Sophocles' *Philoctetes* was performed by academic groups in 1963 and 1978. Cf. Mandel, *Philoctetes*, p. 154, Hartigan, *Greek Tragedy*, p. 145 n. 8.

17. Description by Katherine Mendeloff, 'Theater of War and Healing: The *Philoctetes* Project', unpublished. The text of the play has undergone several stages: there was a workshop version in 1994 based on Sallie Goetsch's translation from the Greek, an adaptation by Brian Spolarich in 1995 for a fuller staging, and another adaptation by Gregory Brandell in 2003.

18. Mendeloff's unpublished paper, delivered in 1994 at the Association for Theater in Higher Education.

19. For the adaptation and use of Greek tragedy as a commentary and response to prevailing political questions, especially towards the end of the twentieth century, see Macintosh, 'Tragedy in Performance', pp. 221-2; Burian, 'Tragedy Adapted for Stages and Screens: the Renaissance to the Present', pp. 282-3. The trend has clearly not stopped there.

20. We may note the Sophoclean allusions in the poem's reference to tourists 'who try taking/ his [Philoctete's] soul with their cameras' (1.I.i) and to Philoctete 'waiting/ to pass out' (1.III.iii), as he had in his spasm.

21. For further discussion of the political implications of the portrayal of Philoctete, see Hardwick, 'Walcott's Philoctete'.

22. For detailed discussion of the ritual and rebirth, see Hamner, *Epic of the Dispossessed: Derek Walcott's Omeros*, pp. 134-8.

23. Hardwick believes that Philoctete's healing is not only individual but social as well. Hardwick, 'Walcott's Philoctete', pp. 102-3.

24. Taplin, 'Sophocles' *Philoctetes*, Seamus Heaney's, and Some Other Recent Half-Rhymes', pp. 147-8.

25. Hartigan, *Greek Tragedy*, p. 150.

Guide to Further Reading

The following guide offers a few selected recommendations for specific fields. For further reading on Greek tragedy and on the *Philoctetes* in particular, please consult the Bibliography.

Translations and commentaries

All the translations of the Greek passages from the play in the book are mine. The following translations of the play have substantial helpful notes for the Greekless reader.

S.L. Schein, *Sophokles: Philoktetes* (Newburyport, MA: Focus Classical Library, 2003) provides a translation with notes, introduction and interpretative essay. J. Affleck, *Sophocles: Philoctetes* (Cambridge: Cambridge University Press, 2001) and C. Phillips, translator, with introduction and notes by D. Clay, *Sophocles: Philoctetes* (New York: Oxford University Press, 2003) do not key their translations to the Greek text's line numbers. D. Grene's translation without notes, *Philoctetes* in D. Grene and R. Lattimore, *Sophocles II* (Chicago and London: University of Chicago Press, 1988) is justly renowned.

Among the following helpful commentaries, Hogan's and Ussher's commentaries do not presuppose knowledge of Greek, Hogan's commentary does not include the text, while Jebb's, Pucci's, and Ussher's commentaries include translations.

J.C. Hogan, *A Commentary on the Plays of Sophocles* (Carbondale and Edwardsville: Southern Illinois University Press, 1991); R.C. Jebb, *Sophocles: The Plays and Fragments. Part IV. The Philoctetes* (London: Bristol Classical Press, 2004 [1898]: the new introduction by F. Budelmann mentions some of the secondary literature on the play); J.C. Kamerbeek, *The Plays of Sophocles*, Part VI, *The Philoctetes* (Leiden: E.J. Brill, 1980); P. Pucci, *Sofocle: Filottete*, introduction and commentary by P. Pucci, text by G. Avezzù and P. Pucci, translation by G. Cerri

(Rome: Fondazione Lorenzo Valla; Milan: A. Mondadori, 2003); R.G. Ussher, *Sophocles: Philoctetes* (Warminster: Aris and Phillips, 1990); T.B.L. Webster, *Sophocles, Philoctetes* (Cambridge: Cambridge University Press, 1970).

Theatre and performance

The following works give an introduction to the available evidence related to the festivals in which Greek drama was performed, issues concerning its performance, staging, and general introduction to Greek tragedy: P. Arnott, *Greek Scenic Conventions in the Fifth Century BC* (Oxford: Clarendon Press, 1962); M. Baldock, *Greek Tragedy, An Introduction* (London: Bristol Classical Press, 1989); E. Csapo and W.J. Slater, *The Context of Ancient Drama* (Ann Arbor: University of Michigan Press, 1995); P.E. Easterling (ed.), *The Cambridge Companion to Greek Tragedy* (Cambridge: Cambridge University Press, 1997); G.H. Gellie, *Sophocles: A Reading* (Carlton, Victoria: Melbourne University Press, 1972); A. Pickard-Cambridge, *The Dramatic Festivals of Athens,* is a classic, the 2nd ed. (Oxford: Clarendon Press, 1968) is revised by J. Gould and D.M. Lewis; O. Taplin, *Tragedy in Action* (Berkeley and Los Angeles: University of California Press, 1978) is among O. Taplin's well known works on the staging of Greek drama; D. Wiles, *Tragedy in Athens: Performance Space and Theatrical Meaning* (Cambridge: Cambridge University Press, 1997) is an illuminating work.

Reception

The most useful resource for the reception of the *Philoctetes* is the Oxford archive for performance http://www.apgrd.ox.ac.uk/. Mandel's work, *Philoctetes and the Fall of Troy* (Lincoln and London: University of Nebraska, 1981), is a good resource for both the mythic variants and reception in literature and art up to 1981. T.E. Rush's MA thesis, 'Modern Interpretations of Sophocles' *Philoctetes*' (Clemson University, 1986), complements Mandel's and brings it up to 1986. Several other works give helpful information about performances and address the play's reception from a variety of points of view: P. Burian, 'Tragedy Adapted for Stages and Screens: the Renaissance to the Present' in P.E. Easterling (ed.), *The Cambridge Companion to Greek Tragedy* (Cambridge: Cambridge University Press, 1997); S. Deane, 'Field Day's Greeks (and Russians)', in M. MacDonald and J.M. Walton (eds) *Amid Our Troubles* (London: Methuen, 2002); H. Flashar, *Inszenierung der Antike: das griechische Drama auf der Bühne der Neuzeit 1585-1990* (Munich: C.H. Beck, 1991); L. Hardwick, 'Walcott's Philoctete: Imaging the Post Colonial Condition' in *Translating Words,*

Translating Cultures (London: Duckworth, 2000); 'Reception as Simile: The Poetics of Reversal in Homer and Derek Walcott', *International Journal of the Classical Tradition* vol. 3 (winter 1997), 326-38; K.V. Hartigan, *Greek Tragedy on the American Stage: Ancient Drama in the Commercial Theater, 1882-1994* (Westport, CT: Greenwood Press, 1995); S. Heaney, 'The Cure at Troy: Production Notes in No Particular Order', in M. MacDonald and J.M. Walton (eds), *Amid Our Troubles* (London: Methuen, 2002); K. Heinemann, *Die tragischen Gestalten der Griechen in der Weltliteratur* (Leipzig: Dieterich, 1920) 2 vols; M. MacDonald and J.M. Walton (eds) *Amid Our Troubles: Irish Versions of Greek Tragedy* (London: Methuen, 2002); F. Macintosh, 'Tragedy in Performance: Nineteenth- and Twentieth-Century Productions' in P.E. Easterling (ed.), *The Cambridge Companion to Greek Tragedy* (Cambridge: Cambridge University Press, 1997); O. Taplin, 'Sophocles' *Philoctetes*, Seamus Heaney's, and Some Other Recent Half-Rhymes', in E. Hall, F. Macintosh, and A. Wrigley (eds) *Dionysus Since 69: Greek Tragedy at the Dawn of the Third Millennium* (Oxford: Oxford University Press, 2004); J.M. Walton, 'Hit or Myth: the Greeks and Irish Drama', in M. MacDonald and J.M. Walton (eds) *Amid Our Troubles* (London: Methuen, 2002).

General Bibliography

F. Ahl, *Sophocles' Oedipus: Evidence and Self-Conviction* (Ithaca and London: Cornell University Press, 1991).

H.C. Avery, 'One Ship or Two at Lemnos?', *Classical Philology* 97 (2002), 1-19.

―――― 'Heracles, Philoctetes, Neoptolemus', Hermes 93 (1965), 279-97.

M. Baldock, *Greek Tragedy, An Introduction* (London: Bristol Classical Press, 1989).

A.G. Beck, *Greek Education: 450-350 BC* (London: Methuen, 1964).

J. Beer, *Sophocles and the Tragedy of Athenian Democracy* (Westport, CT, London: Praeger, 2004).

V. Bers, 'The Perjured Chorus in Sophocles' *Philoctetes*', *Hermes* 109 (1981), 500-4.

J.H. Betts, J.T. Hooker and J.R. Green (eds) *Studies in Honour of T.B.L. Webster*, vol. 1 (Bristol: Bristol Classical Press, 1986).

C.R. Beye, 'Sophocles' *Philoctetes* and the Homeric Embassy', *Transactions and Proceedings of the American Philological Association* 101 (1970), 63-75.

P. Biggs, 'The Disease Theme in Sophocles' *Ajax, Philoctetes* and *Trachiniae*', *Classical Philology* 61 (1966), 223-35.

M.W. Blundell, 'The *Phusis* of Neoptolemus in Sophocles' *Philoctetes*', *Greece & Rome* 35 (1988), 138-48.

―――― 'The Moral Character of Odysseus in *Philoctetes*', *Greek, Roman and Byzantine Studies* 28 (1987), 307-29.

C.M. Bowra, *Sophoclean Tragedy* (Oxford: Oxford University Press, 1965).

P. Burian, 'Tragedy Adapted for Stages and Screens: the Renaissance to the Present', in P.E. Easterling (ed.), *The Cambridge Companion to Greek Tragedy* (Cambridge: Cambridge University Press, 1997), 228-83.

W.M. Calder III, 'Sophoclean Apologia: *Philoctetes*', *Greek, Roman and Byzantine Studies* 12 (1971), 153-74.

A. Cameron, *Greek Mythography in the Roman World* (Oxford, New York: Oxford University Press, 2004).

143

D. Cohen, *Law, Sexuality and Society: The Enforcement of Morals in Classical Athens* (Cambridge: Cambridge University Press, 1994).

E.M. Craik, 'Sophokles and the Sophists', *L'Antiquité Classique* 49 (1980), 247-53.

E. Csapo and W.J. Slater, *The Context of Ancient Drama* (Ann Arbor: University of Michigan Press, 1995).

A.M. Dale, 'Seen and Unseen on the Greek Stage: A Study in Scenic Conventions', in *Collected Papers* (Cambridge: Cambridge University Press, 1969), 119-36.

———— *Collected Papers* (Cambridge: Cambridge University Press, 1969).

M. Damen, 'Actor and Character in Greek Tragedy', *Theatre Journal* 41 (1989), 316-40.

J. Davidson, 'Homer and Sophocles' *Philoctetes*', *Bulletin of the Institute of Classical Studies*, suppl. 66 (1995), 25-35.

S. Deane, 'Field Day's Greeks (and Russians)', in M. MacDonald and J.M. Walton (eds), *Amid Our Troubles* (London: Methuen, 2002), 148-64.

P.E. Easterling , 'Actor as Icon', in P.E. Easterling and E. Hall (eds), *Greek and Roman Actors* (Cambridge: Cambridge University Press, 2002), 327-41.

———— 'Actors and Voices: Reading Between the Lines in Aeschines and Demosthenes', in S. Goldhill and R. Osborne (eds), *Performance Culture and Athenian Democracy* (Cambridge: Cambridge University Press, 1999), 154-66.

———— 'The Tragic Homer', *Bulletin of the Institute of Classical Studies* 31 (1984), 1-8.

———— '*Philoctetes* and Modern Criticism', *Illinois Classical Studies* 3 (1978), 27-39.

———— 'The Transmission of the Text', in T.B.L. Webster, *Sophocles, Philoctetes* (Cambridge: Cambridge University Press, 1970), 164-73.

———— and E. Hall (eds), *Greek and Roman Actors* (Cambridge: Cambridge University Press, 2002).

I. Errandonea, 'Filoctetes', *Emerita* 23 (1955), 122-64; 24 (1956), 72-107.

G. Ferrari, 'Myth and Genre on Athenian Vases', *Classical Antiquity* 22 (2003), 32-54.

H. Flashar, *Inszenierung der Antike: das griechische Drama auf der Bühne der Neuzeit 1585-1990* (Munich: C.H. Beck, 1991).

E. Fraenkel, *Beobachtungen zu Aristophanes* (Rome: Edizioni di Storia e Letteratura, 1962).

C.J. Fuqua, 'The Thematic Structure of Sophocles' *Philoctetes*', Diss. Cornell University, 1964.

C.P. Gardiner, *The Sophoclean Chorus: A Study of Character and Function* (Iowa City: University of Iowa Press, 1987).

R. Garland, *The Greek Way of Death*, 2nd ed. (London: Bristol Classical Press, 2001).

A.F. Garvie, 'Deceit, Violence, and Persuasion in the *Philoctetes*', in *Studi Classici in onore di Quintinio Cataudella* (Catania: Università di Catania, 1972), 213-26.

C. Gill, 'Bow, Oracle, and Epiphany in Sophocles' *Philoctetes*', *Greece & Rome* 27 (1980), 137-46.

S. Goldhill, 'Collectivity and Otherness – The Authority of the Tragic Chorus: Response to Gould', in M.S. Silk (ed.), *Tragedy and the Tragic: Greek Theatre and Beyond* (Oxford: Clarendon Press, 1996), 244-56.

—— 'The Great Dionysia and Civic Ideology', in J.J. Winkler and F.I. Zeitlin (eds), *Nothing to Do with Dionysos? Athenian Drama in its Social Context* (Princeton, NJ: Princeton University Press, 1992), 97-129.

—— *Reading Greek Tragedy* (Cambridge: Cambridge University Press, 1986).

—— and R. Osborne (eds), *Performance Culture and Athenian Democracy* (Cambridge: Cambridge University Press, 1999).

J. Gould, 'Tragedy and Collective Experience', in M.S. Silk (ed.), *Tragedy and the Tragic: Greek Theatre and Beyond* (Oxford: Clarendon Press, 1996), 217-43.

C. Greengard, *Theatre in Crisis: Sophocles' Reconstruction of Genre and Politics in* Philoctetes (Amsterdam: Hakkert, 1987).

J. Griffin, 'Sophocles and the Democratic City', in J. Griffin (ed.), *Sophocles Revisited: Essays Presented to Sir Hugh Lloyd-Jones* (Oxford: Oxford University Press, 1999), 73-94.

—— (ed.), *Sophocles Revisited: Essays Presented to Sir Hugh Lloyd-Jones* (Oxford: Oxford University Press, 1999)

—— 'The Social Function of Attic Tragedy', *Classical Quarterly* 48 (1998), 39-61.

R.E. Grinder, *Adolescence* (New York etc.: John Wiley & Sons, 1978, 2nd ed).

W.K.C. Guthrie, *The Sophists* (Cambridge, etc: Cambridge University Press, 1971).

E. Hall, F. Macintosh and A. Wrigley (eds), *Dionysus Since 69: Greek Tragedy at the Dawn of the Third Millennium* (Oxford: Oxford University Press, 2004).

—— 'The Singing Actors of Antiquity,' in P. Easterling and E. Hall (eds), *Greek and Roman Actors* (Cambridge: Cambridge University Press, 2002), 3-38.

—— 'Actor's Song in Tragedy', in S. Goldhill and R. Osborne (eds),

Performance Culture and Athenian Democracy (Cambridge: Cambridge University Press, 1999), 96-122.

S. Halliwell, 'The Function and Aesthetics of the Greek Tragic Mask', in N.W. Slater & B. Zimmermann (eds), *Drama*, vol. 2: *Intertextualität in der griechisch-römischen Komödie* (Stuttgart: M. und P. Verl. für Wiss. und Forschung, 1993), 195-211.

———— 'Between Public and Private: Tragedy and Athenian Experience of Rhetoric', in C. Pelling (ed.), *Greek Tragedy and the Historian* (Oxford: Clarendon Press, 1977), 121-41.

R.D. Hamner, *Epic of the Dispossessed: Derek Walcott's* Omeros (Columbia and London: University of Missouri Press, 1997).

M.H. Hansen (ed.), *A Comparative Study of Thirty City-State Cultures: An Investigation* [conducted by the Copenhagen Polis Centre] (Copenhagen: Kongelige Danske Videnskabernes Selskab, 2000).

———— *The Athenian Ecclesia, II: A Collection of Articles 1983-89* (Copenhagen: Museum Tusculanum Press, 1989).

L. Hardwick, 'Walcott's Philoctete: Imaging the Post-Colonial Condition', *Translating Words, Translating Cultures* (London: Duckworth, 2000), 97-111.

———— 'Reception as Simile: The Poetics of Reversal in Homer and Derek Walcott', *International Journal of the Classical Tradition*, vol. 3 (winter 1997), 326-38.

K.V. Hartigan, *Greek Tragedy on the American Stage: Ancient Drama in the Commercial Theater, 1882-1994* (Westport, CT: Greenwood Press, 1995).

S. Heaney, '*The Cure at Troy*: Production Notes in No Particular Order', in M. MacDonald and J.M. Walton (eds), *Amid Our Troubles* (London: Methuen, 2002), 171-80.

M. Heath, 'Sophocles' *Philoctetes*: A Problem Play?', in J. Griffin (ed.), *Sophocles Revisited: Essays Presented to Sir Hugh Lloyd-Jones* (Oxford: Oxford University Press, 1999) 137-60.

G. Herman, *Ritualised Friendship and the Greek City* (Cambridge: Cambridge University Press, 1987).

J. Hesk, *Sophocles: Ajax* (London: Duckworth, 2003).

A.E. Hinds, 'The Prophecy of Helenus in Sophocles' *Philoctetes*', *Classical Quarterly* 61 (1967), 169-80.

J.C. Hogan, *A Commentary on the Plays of Sophocles* (Carbondale and Edwardsville: Southern Illinois University Press, 1991).

M.C. Hoppin, 'What Happens in Sophocles' "Philoctetes"?', *Traditio* 37 (1981), 1-30.

S. Humphreys, 'Law, Custom and Culture in Herodotos', *Arethusa* 20 (1987), 211-20.

E. Inoque, 'Sight, Sound, and Rhetoric: *Philoktetes* 29 ff', *American Journal of Philology* 100 (1979), 217-27.

M.H. Jameson, 'Politics and the *Philoctetes*', *Classical Philology* 51 (1956), 217-27.

R.C. Jebb, *Sophocles: The Plays and Fragments. Part IV. The Philoctetes* (London: Bristol Classical Press, 2004 [1898]).

M. Kaimio, *Physical Contact in Greek Tragedy: A Study of Stage Conventions* (Helsinki: Suomalainein Tiedeakatemia, 1988).

J.C. Kamerbeek, *The Plays of Sophocles*. Part VI, *The Philoctetes* (Leiden: E.J. Brill, 1980).

G.A. Kennedy, trans. *Aristotle. On Rhetoric: A Theory of Civic Discourse* (Oxford, New York: Oxford University Press, 1991).

—— *The Art of Persuasion in Greece* (Princeton, NJ: Princeton University Press, 1963).

K.C. King, *Achilles: Paradigms of the War Hero from Homer to the Middle Ages* (Berkeley: University of California Press, 1987).

G.M. Kirkwood, *A Study of Sophoclean Drama* (Ithaca, NY: Cornell University Press, 1958).

J. Kittmer, 'Sophoclean Sophistics: A Reading of Philoktetes', *Materiali e discussioni per l'analisi dei testi classici* 34 (1995), 9-35.

B.M.W. Knox, *The Heroic Temper: Studies in Sophoclean Tragedy* (Berkeley and Los Angeles: University of California Press, 1964).

D. Konstan, *Pity Transformed* (London: Duckworth, 2001).

—— *Friendship in the Classical World* (Cambridge: Cambridge University Press, 1997).

J. Kott, *The Eating of the Gods: An Interpretation of Greek Tragedy* (New York: Vintage Books, 1973).

R. Lattimore, *Story Patterns in Greek Tragedy* (London: The Athlone Press, 1964).

A. Lesky, *Greek Tragic Poetry*, trans. M. Dillon (New Haven and London: Yale University Press, 1983).

—— *A History of Greek Literature*, trans. J. Willis and C. de Heer (New York: Crowell, 1966).

Lexicon Iconographicum Mythologiae Classicae (LIMC), vols VII.1 & 2 (Zürich: Artemis, 1994).

I.M. Linforth, 'Philoctetes: The Play and the Man', *University of California Publications in Classical Philology* 15 (1956), 95-156.

M. MacDonald and J.M. Walton, *Amid Our Troubles: Irish Versions of Greek Tragedy* (London: Methuen, 2002).

F. Macintosh, 'Tragedy in Performance: Nineteenth- and Twentieth-Century Productions', in P.E. Easterling (ed.), *The Cambridge Companion to Greek Tragedy* (Cambridge: Cambridge University Press, 1997), 284-323.

O. Mandel, *Philoctetes and the Fall of Troy* (Lincoln, NE and London: University of Nebraska, 1981).

H.I. Marrou, *A History of Education in Antiquity*, trans. G. Lamb (New York: A Mentor Book, 1964).

147

General Bibliography

C.W. Marshall, 'Some Fifth-Century Masking Conventions', *Greece & Rome* 96 (1999), 188-202.

P. Michelakis, *Achilles in Greek Tragedy* (Cambridge: Cambridge University Press, 2002).

L.A. Milani, *Nuovi Monumenti di Filottete* (Rome: Coltipi del Salviucci, 1882).

—— *Il Mito di Filottete nella Letteratura classica e nell' Arte Figurata* (Florence: Università di Firenze, 1879).

H.W. Miller, 'ὁ φιλόμηρος Σοφοκλῆς (*ho philomêros Sophoklês*) and Eustathius', *Classical Philology* 41 (1946), 99-102.

R. Minadeo, 'Theme and Plot in the *Philoctetes*', *Studi Italiani di Filologia Classica* 11 (1993), 87-105.

J.-C. Moretti, 'The Theater of the Sanctuary of Dionysus Eleuthereus in Late Fifth-Century Athens', *Illinois Classical Studies* 24-5 (1999-2000), 377-98.

I. Morris and B. Powell, *A New Companion to Homer* (Leiden, New York, Köln: Brill, 1997).

C.W. Müller, *Euripides: Philoktet; Testimonien und Fragmente* (Berlin: De Gruyter, 2000).

—— *Philoktete: Beiträge zur Widergewinnung einer Tragödie des Euripides aus der Geschichte ihrer Rezeption* (Stuttgart and Leipzig: B.G. Teubner, 1997).

O. Murray and S. Price (eds), *The Greek City: From Homer to Alexander* (Oxford: Clarendon Press, 1990).

M. Nussbaum, 'Consequences and Character in Sophocles' *Philoctetes*', *Philology and Literature* 1 (1976-77), 25-53.

D. O'Higgins, 'Narrators and Narrative in the *Philoctetes* of Sophocles', *Ramus* 20 (1991), 37-52.

J. Ober, *Mass and Elite in Democratic Athens: Rhetoric, Ideology and the Power of the People* (Princeton, NJ: Princeton University Press, 1989).

M. Oswyn and Simon Price (eds), *The Greek City from Homer to Alexander* (Oxford: Clarendon Press, 1990).

Oxford Archive for Performance http://www.apgrd.ox.ac.uk/.

R. Parker, 'Through a Glass Darkly: Sophocles and the Divine', in J. Griffin (ed.), *Sophocles Revisited: Essays Presented to Sir Hugh Lloyd-Jones* (Oxford: Oxford University Press, 1999), 11-30.

Z. Pavlovskis, 'The Voice of the Actor in Greek Tragedy', *Classical World* 71 (1977), 113-23.

C. Pelling, 'Conclusion', in C. Pelling (ed.), *Greek Tragedy and the Historian* (Oxford: Clarendon Press, 1977), 213-24.

—— (ed.), *Greek Tragedy and the Historian* (Oxford: Clarendon Press, 1997).

A. Pickard-Cambridge, *The Dramatic Festivals of Athens,* 2nd ed.

revised by J. Gould and D.M. Lewis (Oxford: Clarendon Press, 1968).

A.J. Podlecki, 'The Power of the Word in Sophocles' *Philoctetes*', *Greek, Roman and Byzantine Studies* 7 (1966), 233-50.

P. Pucci, 'God's Intervention and Epiphany in Sophocles', *American Journal of Philology* 115 (1994), 15-46.

A.E. Raubitschek, 'A Note on the *Philoctetes* (1402)', in J.H. Betts, J.T. Hooker & J.R. Green (eds), *Studies in Honour of T.B.L. Webster*, vol. 1 (Bristol: Bristol Classical Press, 1986), 198-9.

R. Rehm, *The Play of Space: Spatial Transformation in Greek Tragedy* (Princeton and Oxford: Princeton University Press, 2002).

——— *Radical Theatre: Greek Tragedy and the Modern World* (London: Duckworth, 2003).

M. Robertson, *The Art of Vase-Painting in Classical Athens* (Cambridge, New York: Cambridge University Press, 1992).

D.B. Robinson, 'Topics in Sophocles' *Philoctetes*', *Classical Quarterly* 19 (1969), 34-56.

H.M. Roisman, 'Nestor the Good Counsellor', *Classical Quarterly* 55 (2005) 1-23.

——— 'Teiresias, the Seer of *Oedipus the King*: Sophocles' and Seneca's Versions', *Liverpool International Classical Seminar* 2.5 (2003), 1-20 (http://www.leeds.ac.uk/classics/lics/)

——— 'The Ever-Present Odysseus: Eavesdropping and Disguise in Sophocles' *Philoctetes*', *Eranos* 99 (2001), 38-53.

——— 'The Appropriation of a Son: Sophocles' *Philoctetes*', *Greek, Roman and Byzantine Studies* 38 (1997), 127-71.

——— *Loyalty in Early Greek Epic and Tragedy* (Königstein/Ta.: Hain, 1984).

J. Roisman, *Rhetoric of Manhood: Masculinity in the Attic Orators* (Berkeley: University of California Press, 2005).

P.W. Rose, *Sons of the Gods, Children of Earth* (Ithaca, NY and London: Cornell University Press, 1992), 273-327 = 'Sophocles' *Philoctetes* and the Teachings of the Sophists', *Harvard Studies in Classical Philology* 80 (1976), 49-105.

T.E. Rush, 'Modern Interpretations of Sophocles' *Philoctetes*', MA thesis, Clemson University, 1986.

M. Ryzman, 'Neoptolemos' Psychological Crisis and the Development of Physis in Sophocles' *Philoctetes*', *Eranos* 89 (1991), 35-41.

C. Segal, *Tragedy and Civilization: An Interpretation of Sophocles* (Cambridge, Mass.: Published for Oberlin College by Harvard University Press, 1981).

S.C. Shucard, 'Some Developments in Sophocles' Late Plays of Intrigue', *Classical Journal* 69 (1973), 133-8.

M.S. Silk (ed.), *Tragedy and the Tragic: Greek Theatre and Beyond* (Oxford: Clarendon Press, 1996).

N.W. Slater & B. Zimmermann (eds), *Drama* vol. 2: *Intertextualität in der griechisch-römischen Komödie* (Stuttgart: M. und P. Verl. für Wiss. und Forschung, 1993).

A.H. Sommerstein, *Greek Drama and Dramatists* (London; New York: Routledge, 2002).

O. Taplin, 'Sophocles' *Philoctetes*, Seamus Heaney's, and Some Other Recent Half-Rhymes', in E. Hall, F. Macintosh, and A. Wrigley (eds), *Dionysus Since 69: Greek Tragedy at the Dawn of the Third Millennium* (Oxford: Oxford University Press, 2004), 146-67.

—— 'Comedy and the Tragic', in M.S. Silk (ed.), *Tragedy and the Tragic: Greek Theatre and Beyond* (Oxford: Clarendon Press, 1996), 188-202.

—— 'The Mapping of Sophocles' *Philoctetes*,' *Bulletin of the Institute of Classical Studies* 34 (1987), 69-77.

—— *Tragedy in Action* (Berkeley and Los Angeles: University of California Press, 1978).

—— *The Stagecraft of Aeschylus: The Dramatic Use of Exits and Entrances in Greek Tragedy* (Oxford: Clarendon Press, 1977).

—— 'Significant Actions in Sophocles' *Philoctetes*', *Greek, Roman and Byzantine Studies* 12 (1971), 25-44.

S. Usher, *Greek Oratory: Tradition and Originality* (Oxford: Oxford University Press, 1999).

R.G. Ussher, *Sophocles: Philoctetes* (Warminster: Aris & Phillips, 1990).

H. van Wees, 'Homeric Warfare', in I. Morris and B. Powell (eds), *A New Companion to Homer* (Leiden, New York, Köln: Brill, 1997), 668-93.

J.P. Vernant and P. Vidal-Naquet, *Myth and Tragedy in Ancient Greece*, trans. J. Lloyd (New York: Zone Books, 1988).

M. Vickers, 'Alcibiades on Stage: *Philoctetes* and *Cyclops*', *Historia* 36 (1987), 171-97.

P. Vidal-Naquet, 'Sophocles' *Philoctetes* and the Ephebeia', in J-P. Vernant and P. Vidal-Naquet, *Myth and Tragedy in Ancient Greece*, trans. J. Lloyd (New York: Zone Books, 1988), 161-79.

—— *The Black Hunter: Forms of Thought and Forms of Society in the Greek World*, trans. A. Szegedy-Maszak (Baltimore and London: Johns Hopkins University Press, 1986).

A.J.A. Waldock, *Sophocles the Dramatist* (Cambridge: Cambridge University Press, 1951).

J.M. Walton, 'Hit or Myth: the Greeks and Irish Drama', in M. MacDonald and J.M. Walton (eds), *Amid Our Troubles* (London: Methuen, 2002), 3-36.

T.B.L. Webster, *Sophocles, Philoctetes* (Cambridge: Cambridge University Press, 1970).

M. Whitby, 'Telemachus Transformed? The Origins of Neoptolemus in Sophocles' *Philoctetes*', *Greece & Rome* 43 (1996), 31-42.

T. von Wilamowitz-Moellendorff, *Die dramatischen Technik des Sophokles* (Hildesheim: Weidmann, 1966 [1917]).

D. Wiles, *Tragedy in Athens: Performance Space and Theatrical Meaning* (Cambridge: Cambridge University Press, 1997).

E. Wilson, 'Philoctetes: The Wound and the Bow', in *The Wound and the Bow: Seven Studies in Literature* (New York: Oxford University Press, 1947), 272-95.

—— *The Wound and the Bow: Seven Studies in Literature* (New York: Oxford University Press, 1947).

P. Wilson, *The Athenian Institution of the* Khoregia (Cambridge: Cambridge University Press, 2000).

J.J. Winkler and F.I. Zeitlin (eds), *Nothing to Do with Dionysos? Athenian Drama in its Social Context* (Princeton, NJ: Princeton University Press, 1992).

M.M. Winkler, 'The Face of Tragedy: From Theatrical Mask to Cinematic Close-Up', *Mouseion* 2 (2002), 43-70.

R.P. Winnington-Ingram, *Sophocles: An Interpretation* (Cambridge: Cambridge University Press, 1980).

www.english.emory.edu/Bahri/FieldDay/html

G. Xanthakis-Karamanos, *Studies in Fourth-Century Tragedy* (Athens: Akademia Athenon, 1980).

Glossary

Archon eponymos. Official who, among other things, selected the three tragedians to compete in the City Dionysia festival.

Aretê. Virtue, kindness, excellence, nobility.

Atreids. Sons of Atreus: Agamemnon and Menelaos.

Boulê. The elected council that set the agenda for the assembly.

Chorêgos/chorêgoi. Producer(s).

City Dionysia (or **Great Dionysia**). Annual state-sponsored festival in Athens in which tragedies were performed.

Dêmos. The people, citizen-body.

Deus ex machina. 'God from the machine'.

Eisodos see *parodos*.

Ekkyklêma. Wooden platform on wheels.

Epeisodion (plural: *epeisodia*). Act(s) of the play between choral odes.

Ephebes. Young men of military age.

Ergon. Action, deed.

Exodos. Final part of the play following a choral ode.

Hyperêtein. To row.

Kommos. Lyric dialogue between the Chorus and a key character.

Logos. Word, speech, system.

Mêchanê. Crane.

Nomos. Custom, convention, education.

Orchêstra. Dancing place where the chorus performed.

Parodos. Ode the Chorus sing as they enter; one of the two aisles on either side of the *orchêstra* running up to the stage-building.

Physis. Nature.

Prologos. First portion of the play before the entrance of the Chorus.

Skênê. Stage-building.

Skênographia. Scene painting.

Stasimon. Choral song and dance between episodes.

Stichomythia. Rapid exchange of single lines.

Chronology

Index

Bold numbers are used for references to works quoted in the text and notes. All other numbers are references to the page and note numbers of this book.

154

Index